STEAMPUNK

Drawing Amazing

Steampunk Figures!

By Jeffrey Stains

Table of Contents

Disclaimer

While all attempts have been made to verify the information provided in this book, the author does assume any responsibility for errors, omissions, or contrary interpretations of the subject matter contained within. The information provided in this book is for educational and entertainment purposes only. The reader is responsible for his or her own actions and the author does not accept any responsibilities for any liabilities or damages, real or perceived, resulting from the use of this information.

The trademarks that are used are without any consent, and the publication of the trademark is without permission or backing by the trademark owner. All trademarks and brands within this book are for clarifying purposes only and are the owned by the owners themselves, not affiliated with this document.

Introduction

As an avid follower of Steampunk, you might have an idea about the kind of drawings Steampunk consists of. Let us give you a brief introduction about this form of art and how it came to the mainstream. In layman's terms, Steampunk is basically modern laptops, aircrafts, cars etc. set in the backdrop of 1800s.

Steampunk is actually a movement of art inspired from the Victorian Era of England. It is a sub-genre of fantasy and science fiction. It also includes aesthetic designs with technological drawings inspired by the Victorian age or 19th century machinery. This machinery was mainly steam powered. Hence, the name- Steampunk originated. Some people also credit the origin of the term to be derived from the word- Cyberpunk.

This genre may also incorporate elements from other genres like horror, fantasy, historical fiction, speculative fiction etc. All these elements taken together make Steampunk a hybrid genre. It appeared in the mainstream for the first time in 1980s. Apart from being an art form, this style also appears in clothing fashion, visual and musical art forms.

This book aims at teaching you the basics of drawing the Steampunk figures. Our focus is to make these drawings as easy as possible. Though the machinery and gadgets shown in the sketches may appear intimidating at times, but is very easy to move ahead step by step. If we do not make the draft like a freehand task and draw the sketches in chunks, it becomes easy to draw a huge drawing in no time.

We will move ahead chapter by chapter and raise the difficulty level gradually. We will also give you step by step instructions for drawing some illustrations. In the initial stages, it might be difficult for you to adapt with the genre, but after a few chapters, you will find that you have got your hands on with the Steampunk figures.

Part A- Basics

Chapter 1

Basic Steampunk Machines Parts

There are several steam machine parts, which can be drawn easily, once you give in regular practice. Here, in this chapter we have listed a few machine parts that can be conveniently inserted in Steampunk drawings.

Shafts

A line shaft is used to transmit power from one source to another. There are thousands of shafts in millions of machinery in every industry. It is basically an elongated part. You can insert a shaft into your drawings wherever you feel the need.

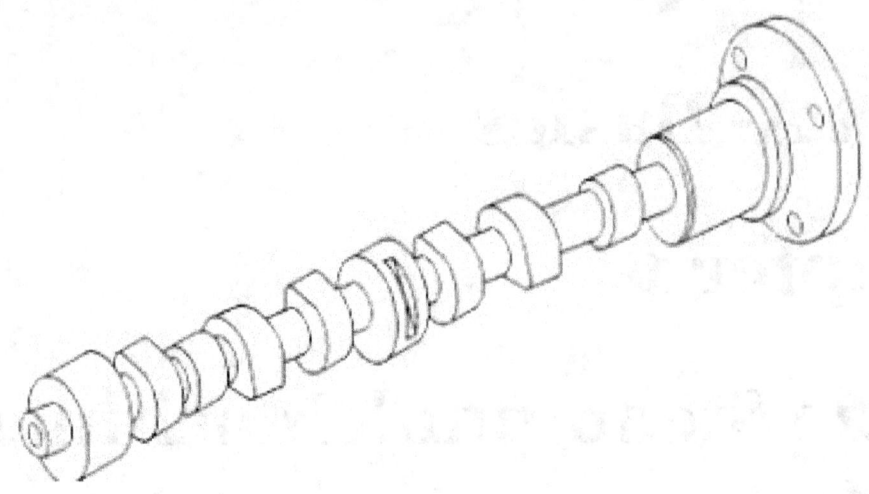

Bearings

A bearing is used to restrict the motion between two moving parts of a machine. It is a very interesting part to be used in Steampunk drawings. The circular design allows you to add a great look to the illustrations.

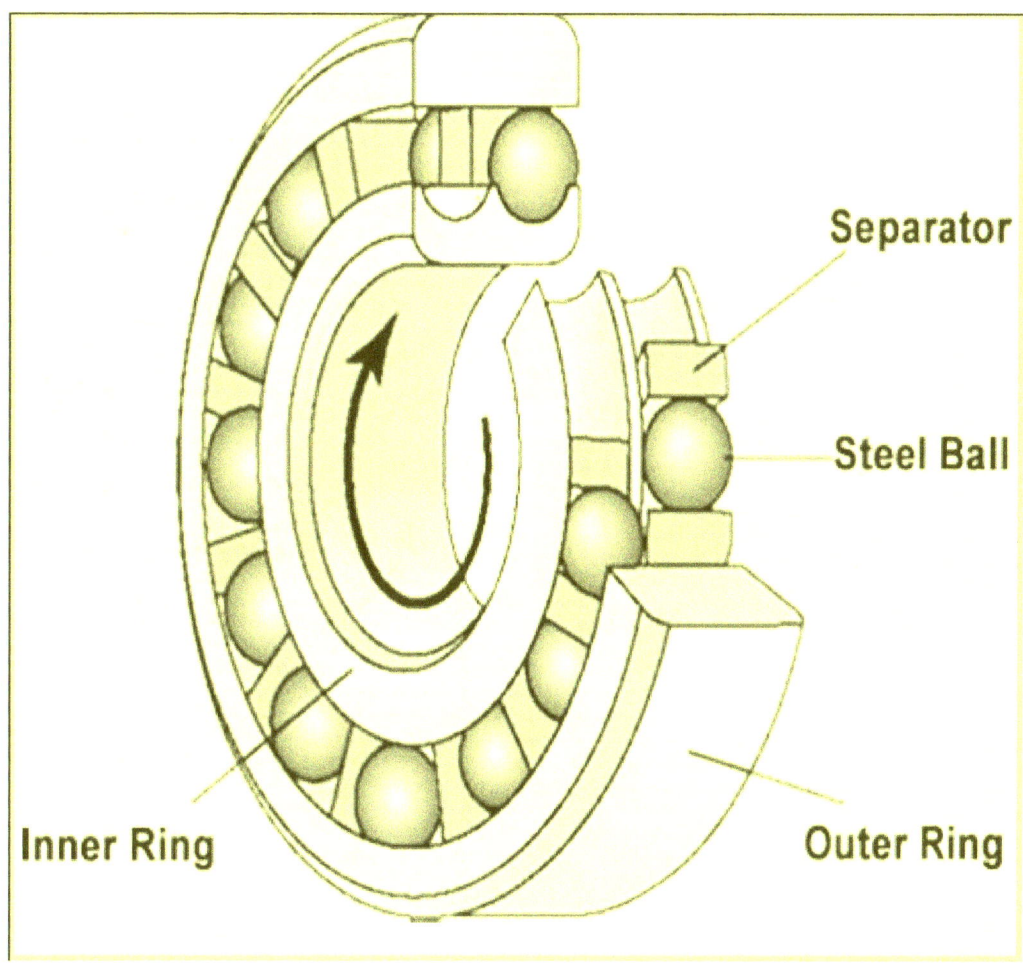

Gear

A gear is a toothed part of a machine, which is used to mesh with other gears to transmit torque. It is also very beautiful part to be inserted in Steampunk drawings. In the drawings that follow, you will see that we have used gears quite often.

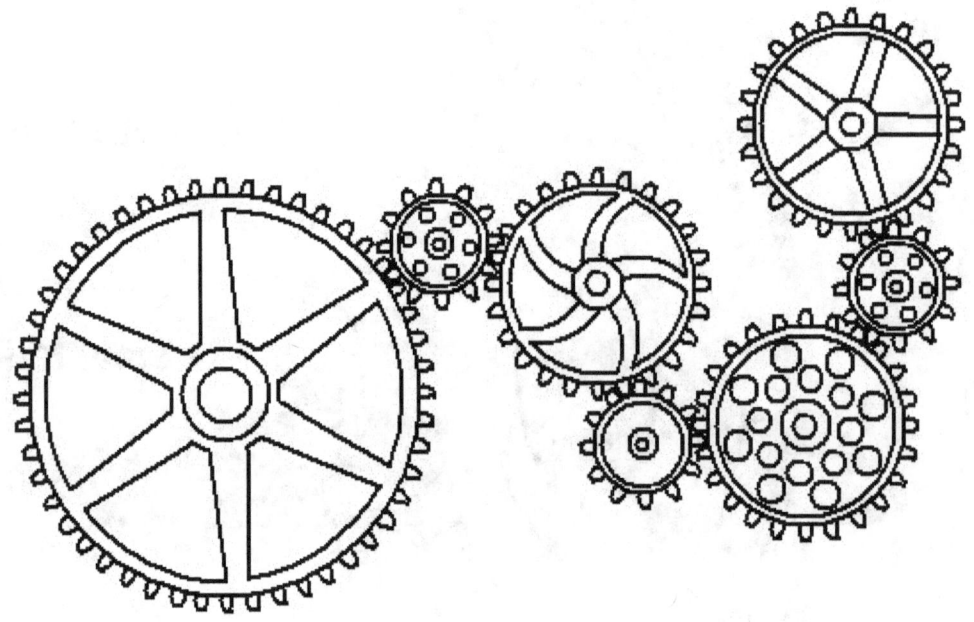

Gear Train

A gear train consists of a few gears that are mounted on a frame in such a way that the teeth of all the gears engage with each other perfectly.

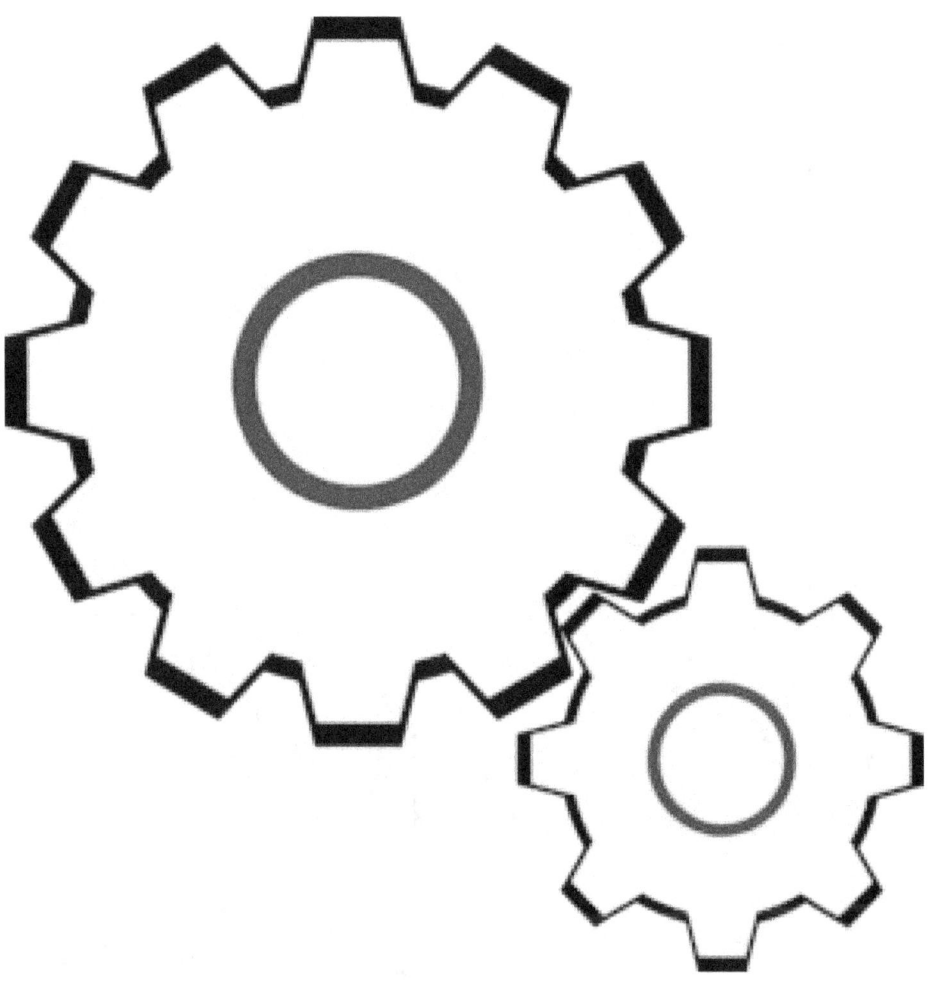

Rivets

A rivet is used to permanently fasten one thing to the other. It consists of a head and a tail. Some of them come with a "+" sign, which can be used in the central parts of some gears as well. The parallel circular drawings on the tail also add amazing features to the drawings. In your illustrations, wherever you feel emptiness, you can insert rivets. It will fulfill the gaps-permanently!

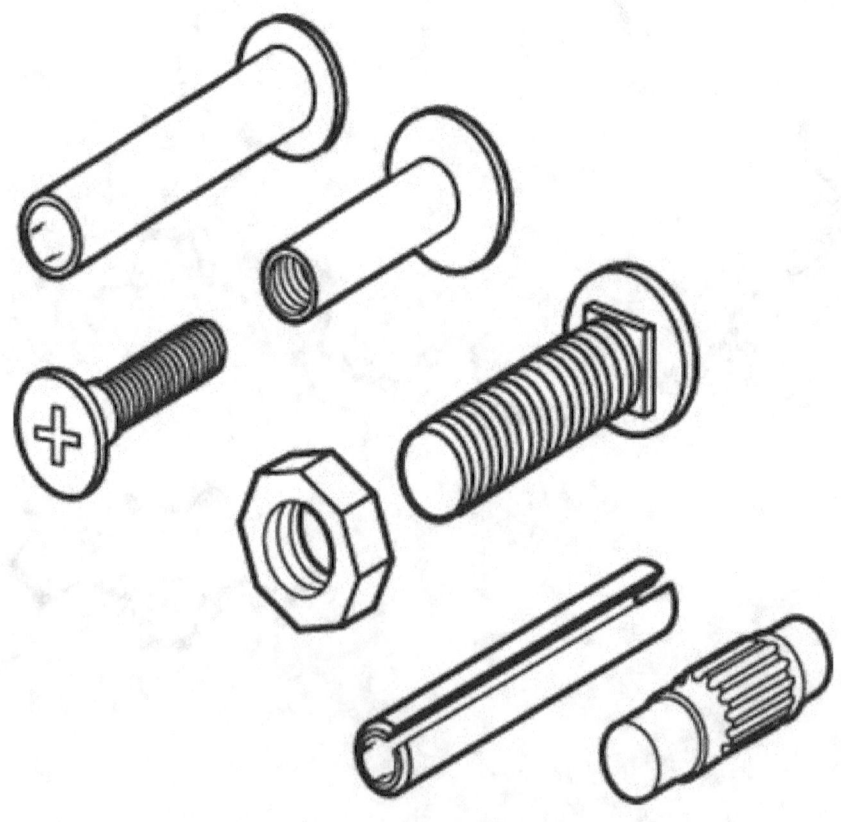

Rack and Pinion

A rack and pinion is a linear actuator which consists of a gear and a gear bar. The gear is called "pinion" and the gear bar is called "rack' in this case. The pinion engages its teeth on the pinion and they move in relative motion in various machines.

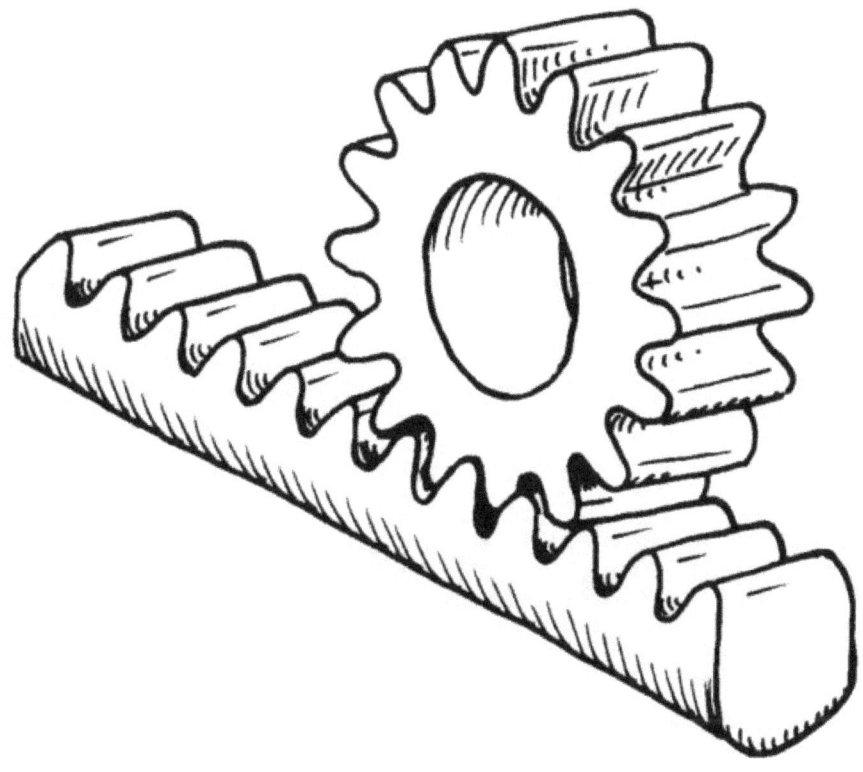

There are thousands of machine parts which can be used for drawing purpose in various genres including steampunk. Basic parts have been listed above. You can also explore different machines in your garage and use them in your artworks. There is no limit to creativity. You never know, you might end up creating a new genre!

Part B- How to draw various Steampunk Illustrations

Chapter 1 - Butterfly

We will start with some basic drawings of the Steampunk genre. Butterfly is one of the most amazing creations of God. Artists have made this creature in millions of forms. And in whatever form we make it, it turns out equally beautiful. We will try to make a butterfly in steampunk.

To make a Steampunk Butterfly, you need to follow these steps:

Step 1

Draw the outline of a butterfly. You can give yourself the liberty to modify the shape of the wings. You can make them diagonal to each other, or in a resting position. Take the help of an "X" to position them opposite to each other.

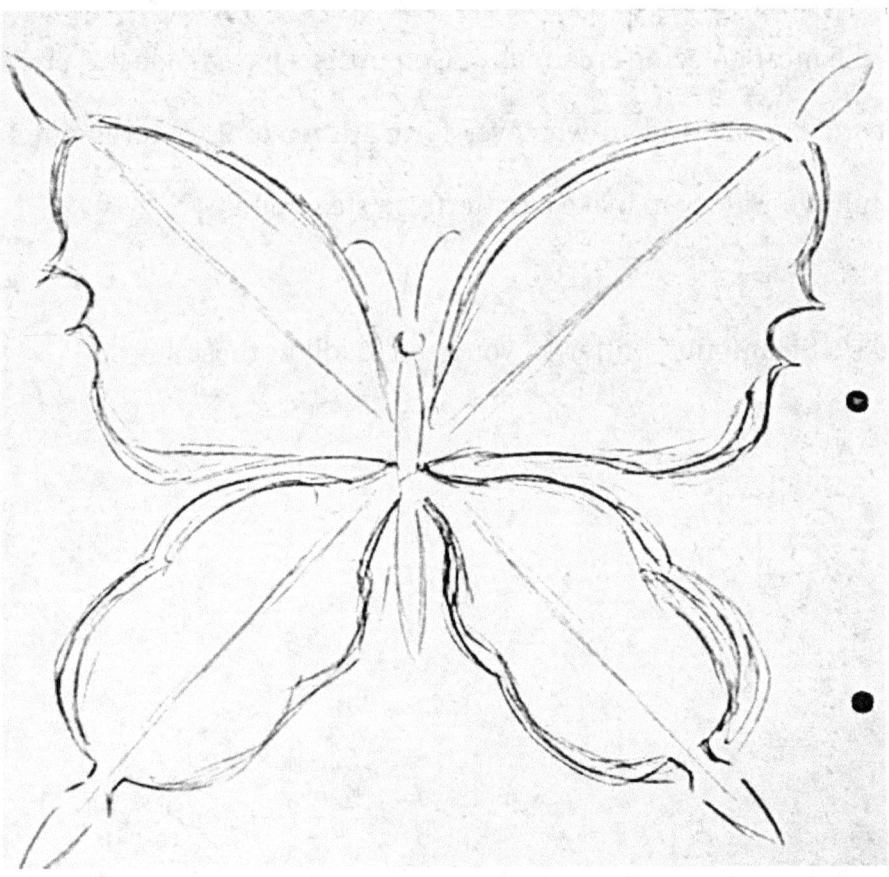

Step 2

You have to move step by step with each body part for detailing. Start with drawing the body of the butterfly. Remember that you are not making a realistic picture of the insect. Keeping the Steampunk genre in mind; draw the head, antennae and rest of the central body using nuts, bolts etc.as intricate details.

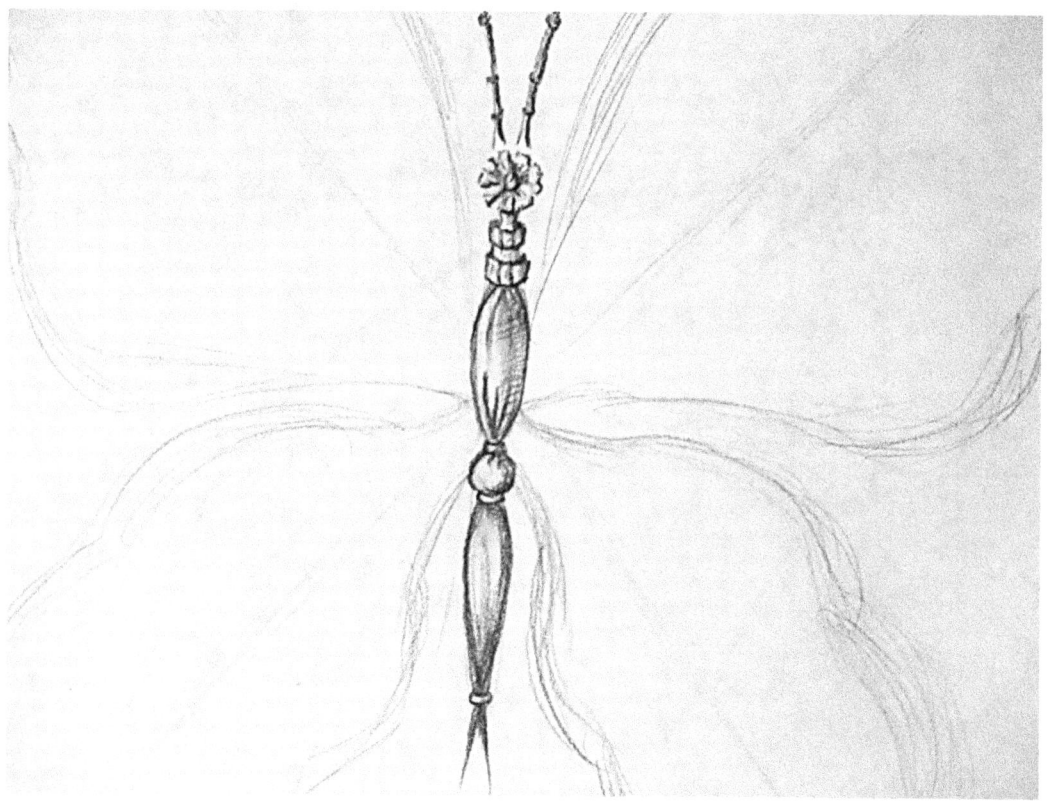

Step 3

Now we will start detailing the top left forewing of the butterfly. Draw the corner of the wing like a spear with a shaft. For adding a smaller circle to the neck of the shaft, draw it in a 3D form as intricately as possible. Simultaneously, draw the outline of the wing with bolder pencil highlights.

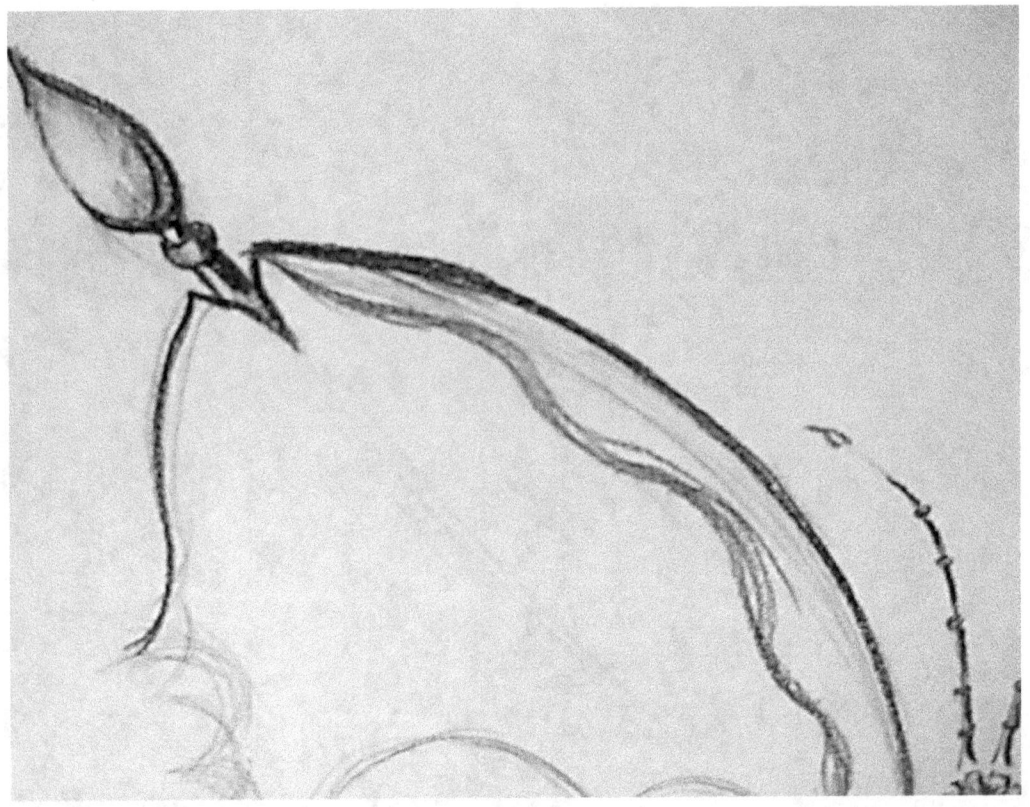

Step 4

The next step is to give a bold outline to the whole figure while keeping it more like a machine rather than an insect. Though the basic ouline should convey that it is a lively butterfly, the details would give a message to the mind that it is a mechanized butterfly. Draw some circles of different sizes inside the wings to draw the gears later, like they are mounted in a gear train.

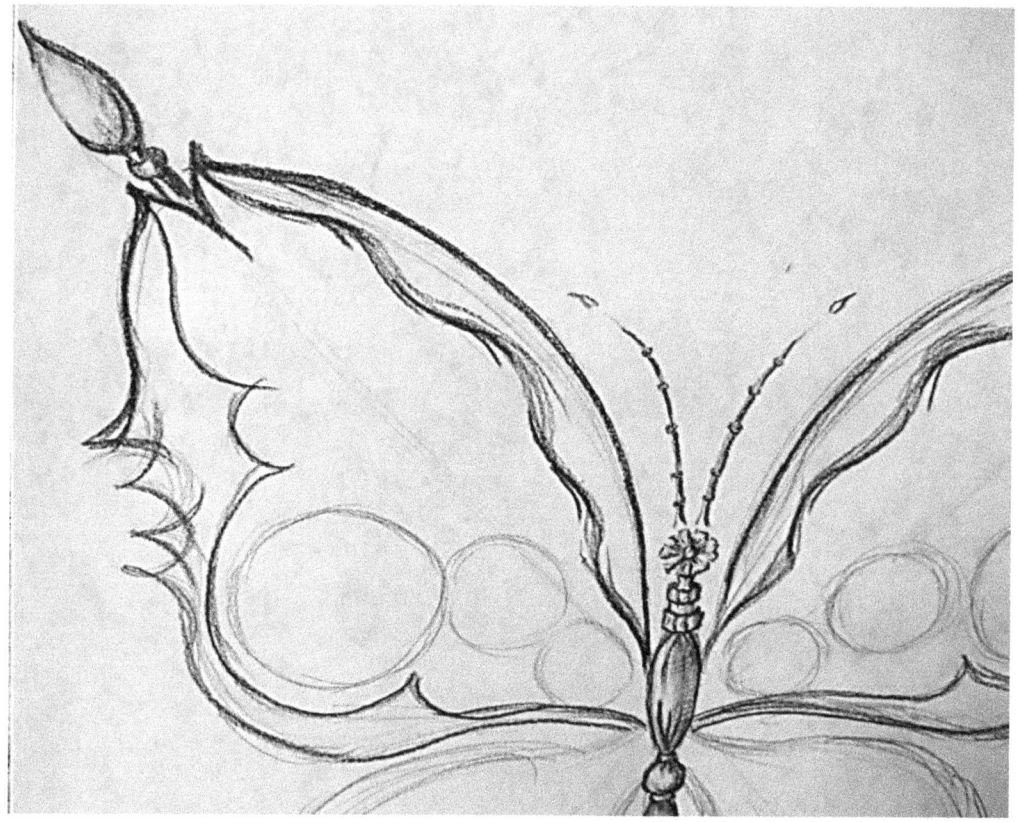

Step 5

Draw the teeth of the gears and their inner details as well. The teeth of the big and small gears should be drawn in conjunction with each other. Along with these parts, draw a few more details in the wings.

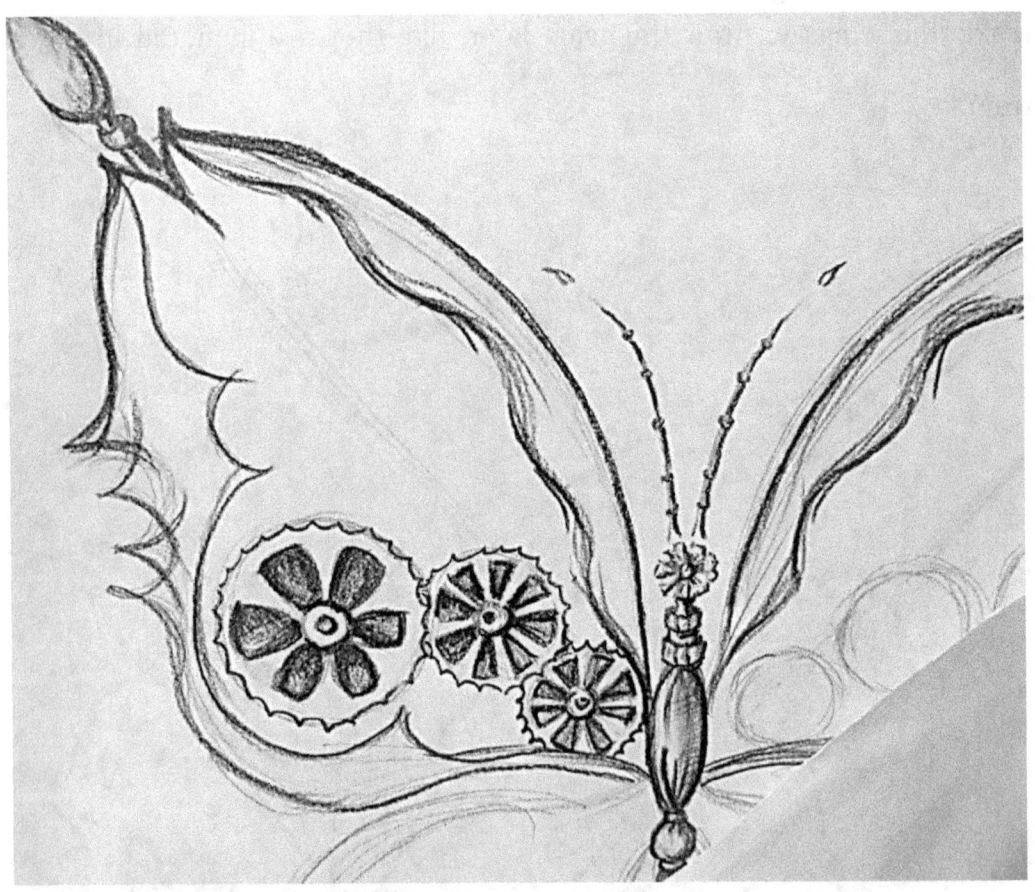

Step 6

Draw lips-like or rose-petal-like drawing inside the wing. It depends upon you how you want to perceive them. To mechanize the lips or the rose petals, add a fastener and a shaft beginning from the petals and ending at the gear.

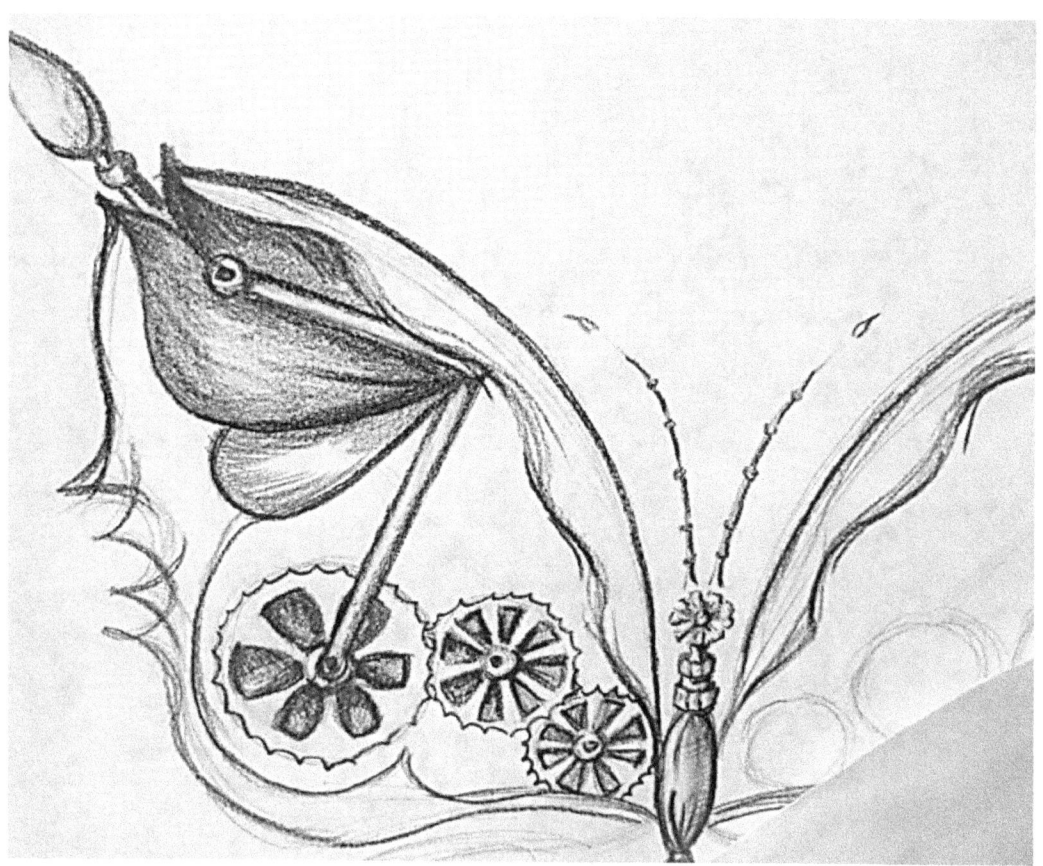

Step 7

Complete the top left forewing with shading the lips or petals and the area surrounding them.

Begin the drawing in the lower left wing. Draw some gears and two shafts.

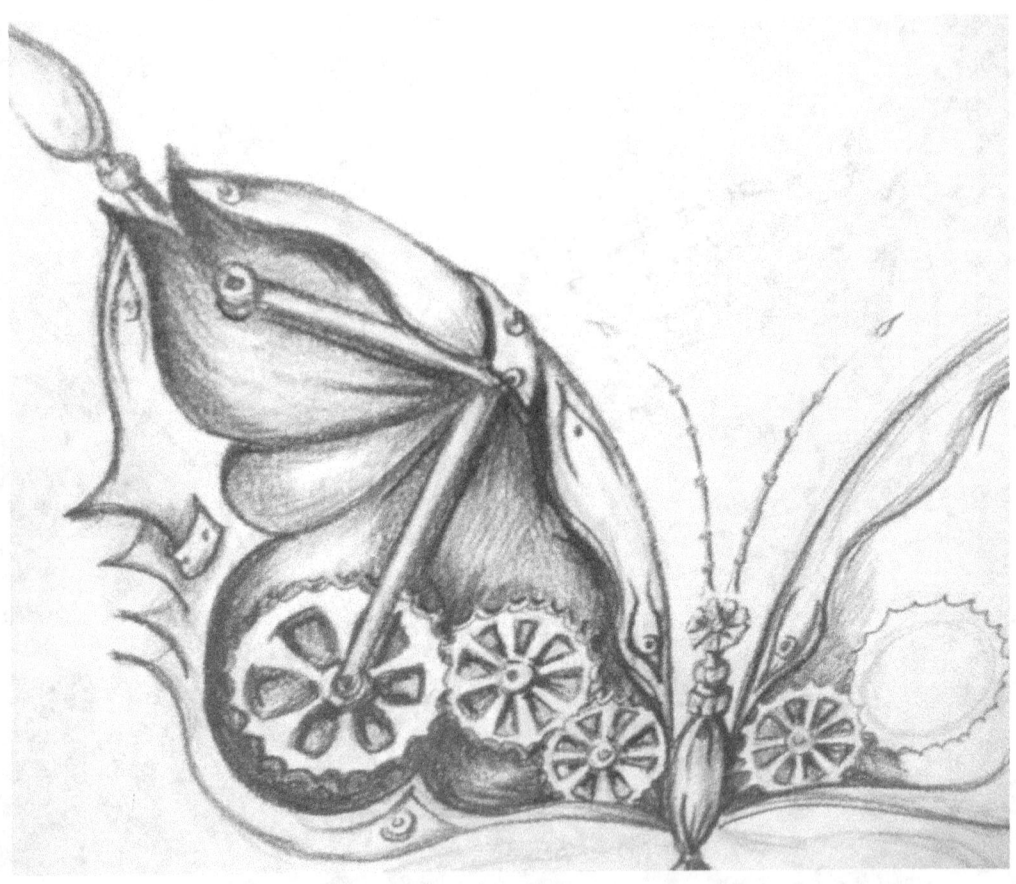

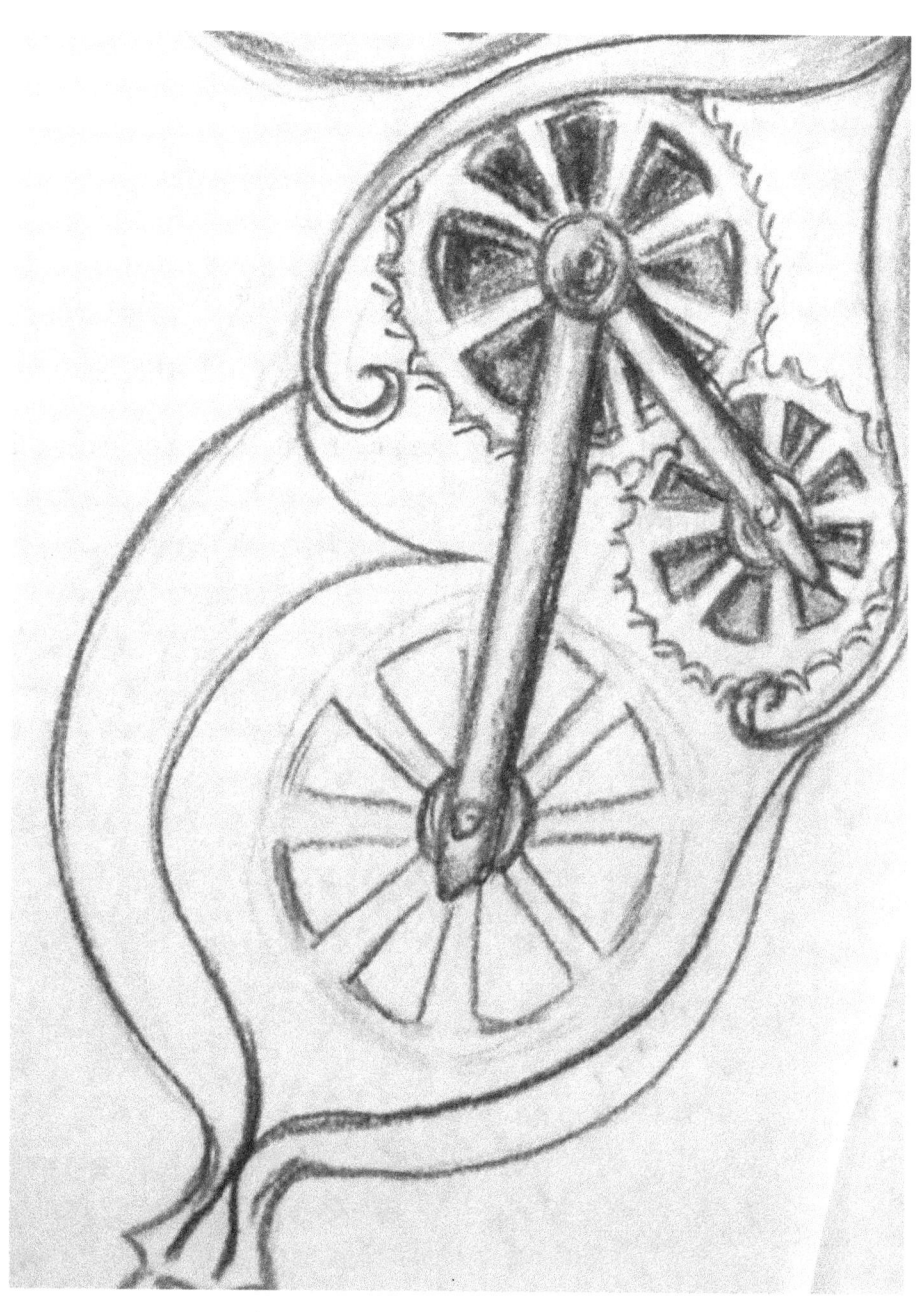

Step 8

When you complete the left wings, they should look like this. Notice the details given in the gears of the lower wing and the saddle type embellishment on the extreme side of the lower left wing. You can add such details depending upon your creativity.

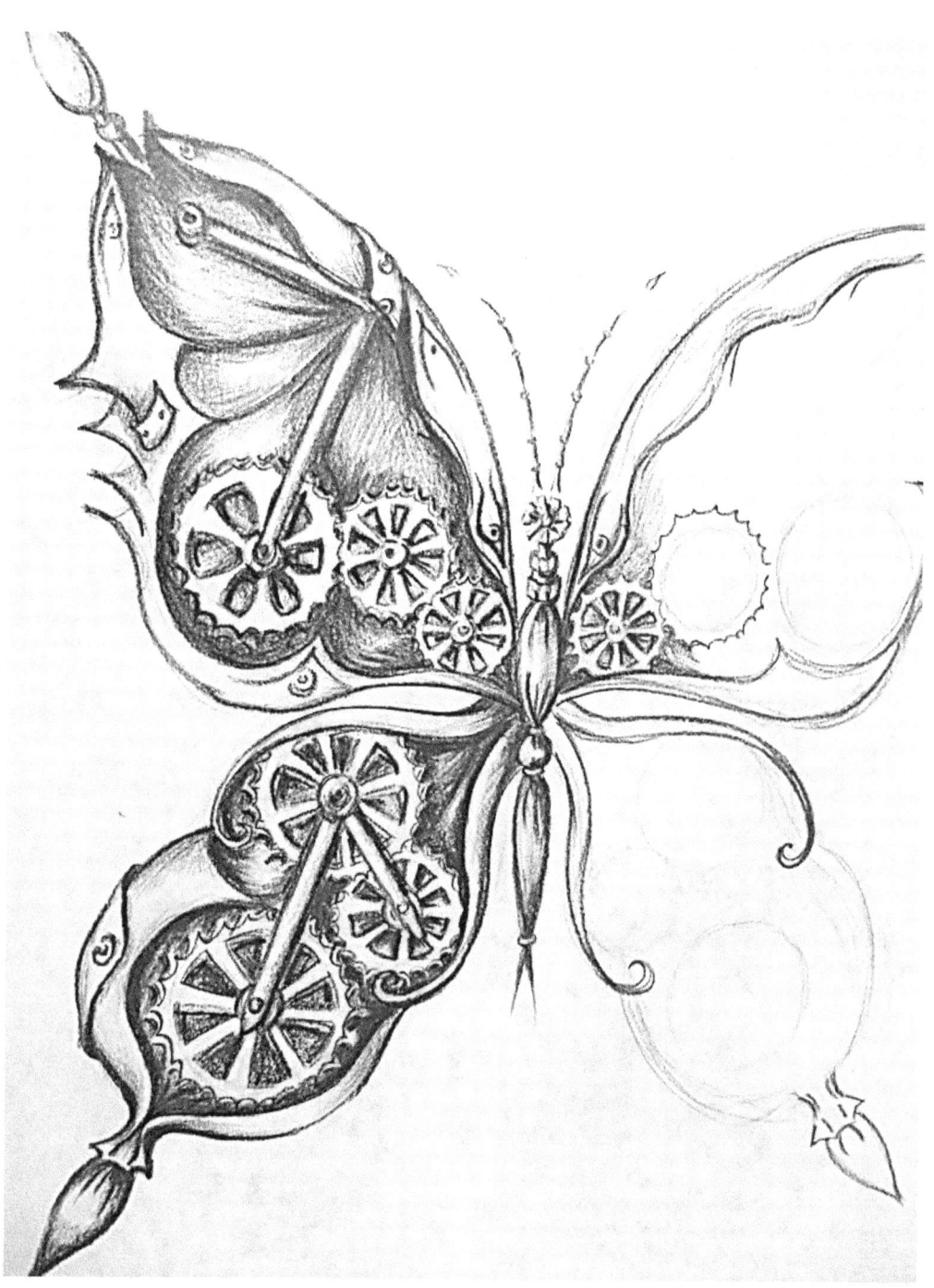

Step 9

In the last step, you have to make the opposite pair of wings as a replica of the set of wings on the left. The Steampunk butterfly is ready.

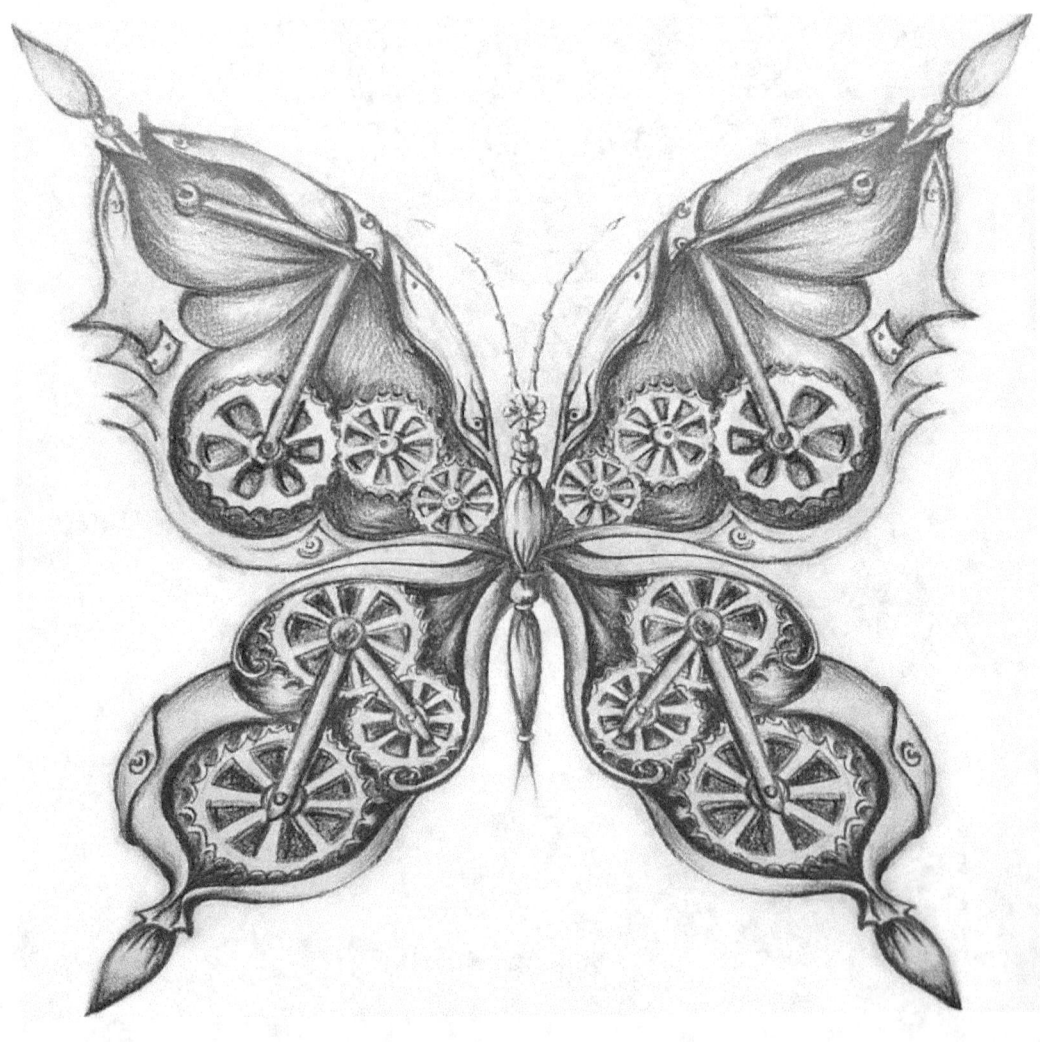

Chapter 2 - An eye

God has gifted many priceless things to humans. Amongall the features of human face, eye is the most adorable feature. It has been illustrated by hundereds of artists in some of the most amazing ways. Sometimes, it seems overwhelming to draw an eye, but it is not so difficult to draw, provided you take care to draw the details one by one. The intricacies of an eye are supposed to be observed very carefully even before you start drawing its outline.

Many artists miss the shine that is visible in every eye if you look closely. Observe the eyes of anyone sitting close to you. You will find that there are many fine lines in this adorable human feature that need to be drawn perfectly. Outside the eyes, between the eyebrows, there are several fine lines, which need to be carefully studied. The eyelashes are turned and twisted in different ways.

Every human being on earth has distinct features, which makes them unique. Even a few minor changes in a face can change the whole personality of a man or a woman. Thus, while drawing eyes, you have to be very careful.

However, here in this chapter, we are going to mix human features and the features of a machine together. The eye we have illustrated, looks like a human eye at first sight. But, the beauty of Steampunk genre is that when the onlookers look closely, the drawing turns out to be a combination of non-human things altogether. So, let us start with the tutorial.

Step 1

Draw the basic outline of an eye very carefully. The eye ball never completely touches the outline of the eye. Do make the mistake of making a complete circle. The eye ball is "slightly" elliptical.

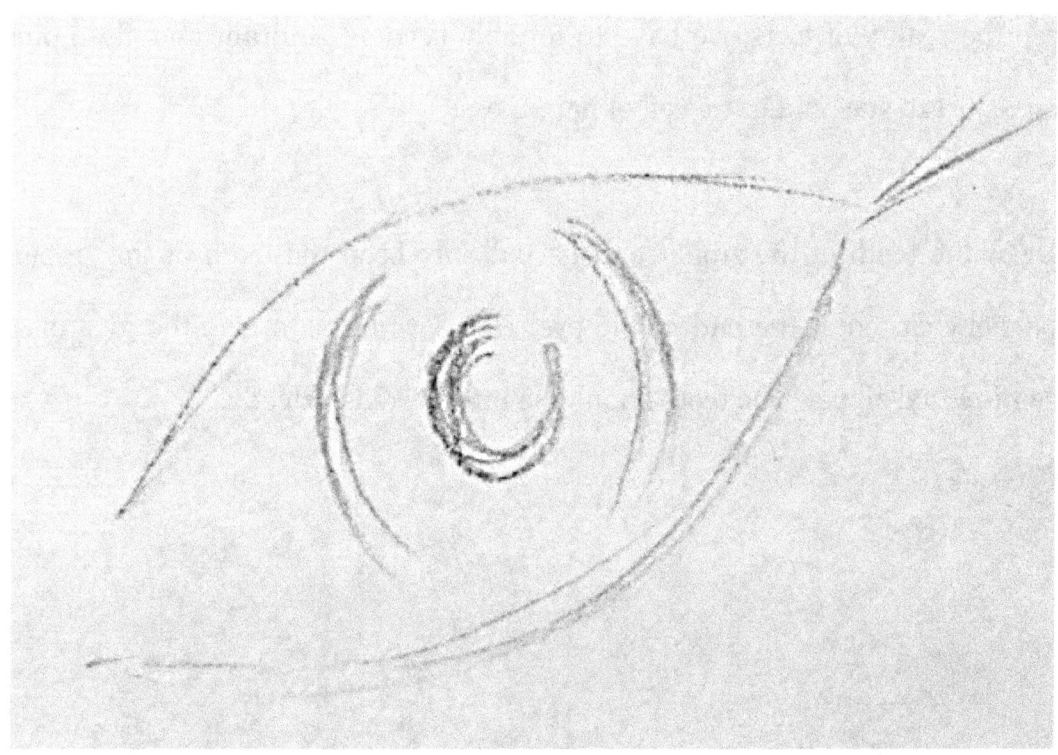

Step 2

We will make this eye like a mechanical eye with a zipper for opening and closing it. The idea behind making it this way is to portray the mechanized human emotions. Sometimes, we have to deliberately open our eyes to face the world, when we do not want to. On the opposite side, when we want to see the reality of facts, we have to forcibly become ignorant and close our eyes, just to stay under the veil of happiness.

Draw the teeth of the zipper and its pull tab. keep the teeth of the zipper partially closed at the end of the eye. Here, we want to give the idea of a semi-closed zipper. The teeth should be interlocked perfectly.

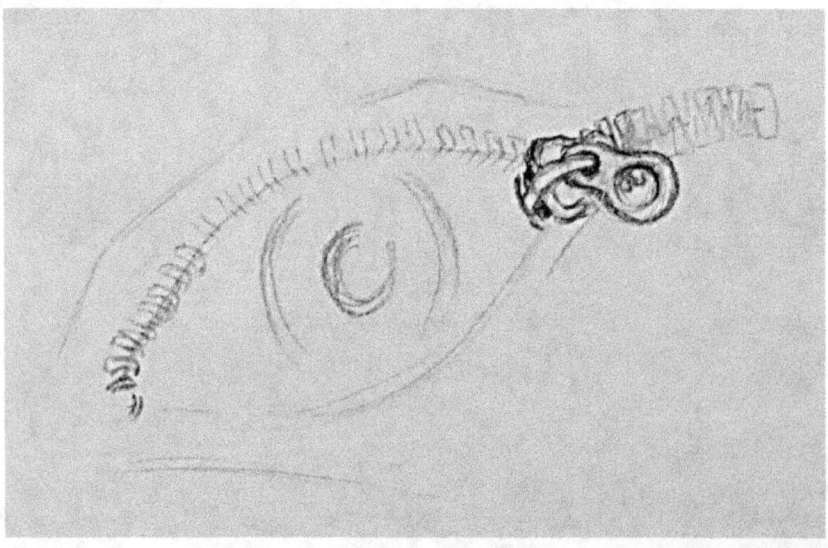

Step 3

Give detailing to the teeth and draw a baseline for them underneath. Highlight the pull tab as well, with bolder lines.

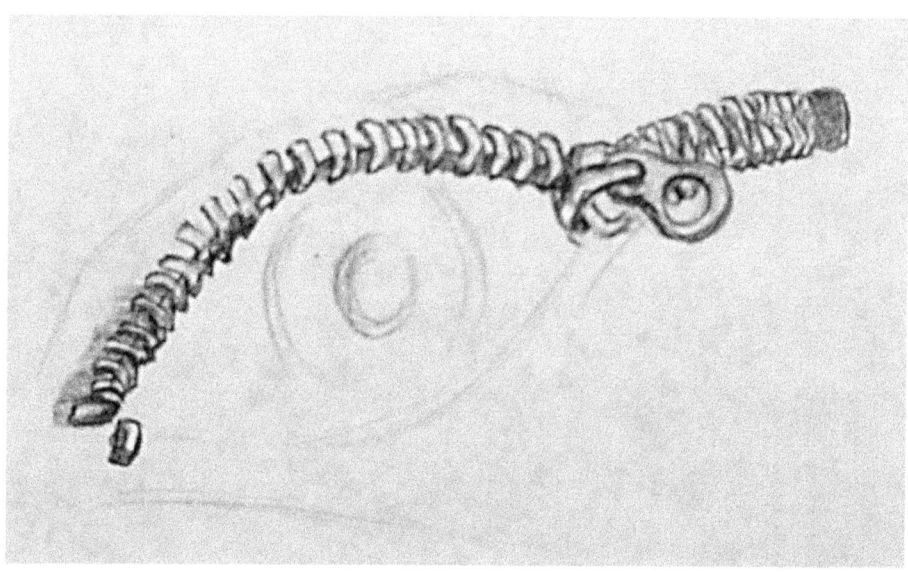

Step 4

Draw the lines that suggest the skin over the "above lid" of the eye. You can also draw the lower line of teeth of the zipper as well, but, with fewer details at this stage. This lower part of the zipper suggests the bottom lid of the eye.

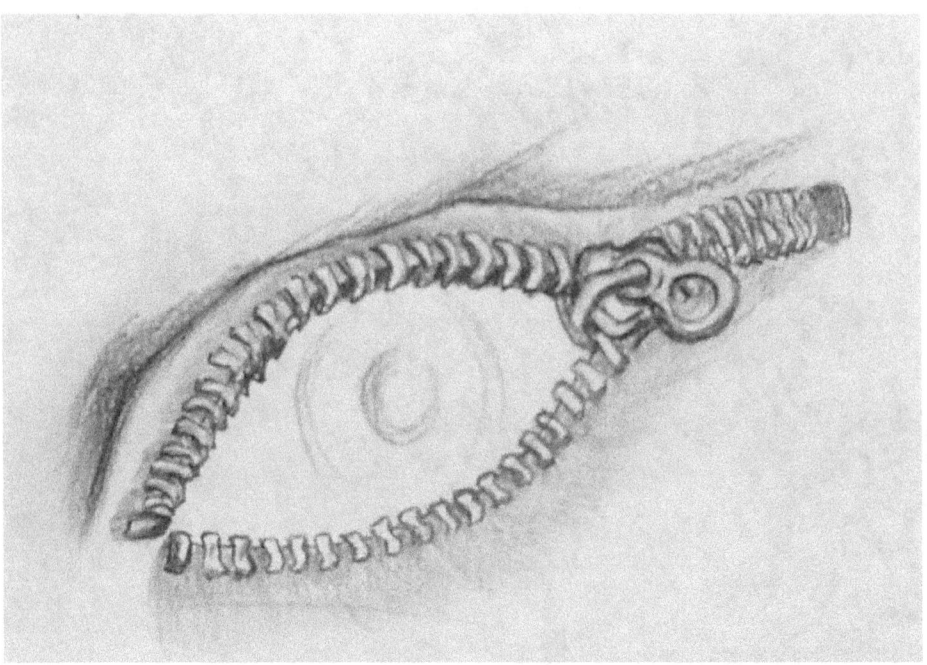

Step 5

Give bold lines and details to the lower line of the zipper. Give the suggestion of some shading beneath the bottom lid of the eyes, i.e. below the lower part of the zipper.

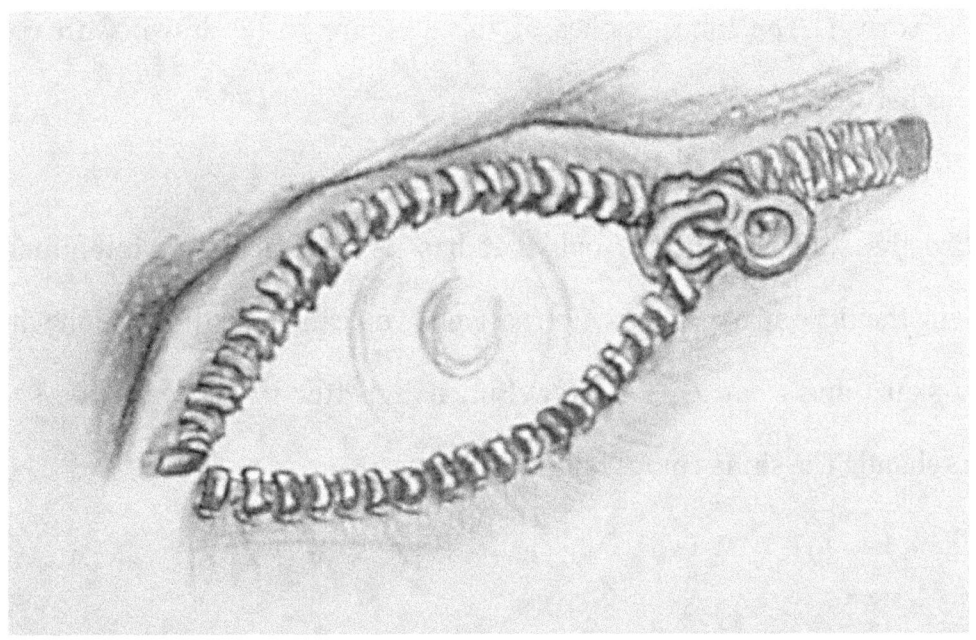

Step 6

Start drawing the gear in place of the eye ball. Draw the central circle of the gear. It is to be drawn as one circle placed on the top of another. Notice the detail of the inner circle. A sign of "+" has been drawn on the rivet to signify the space that is indented in all fasteners for opening and closing them with a screwdriver. The inner spokes of the gear are to be drawn with equal spaces between them.

Notice the shine in the eye ball that has been depicted by intentionally leaving the little space empty. Alternatively, you can erase the portion with a very sharp and clean eraser later. But, it is better if you leave the space beforehand. The shine comes out more neatly.

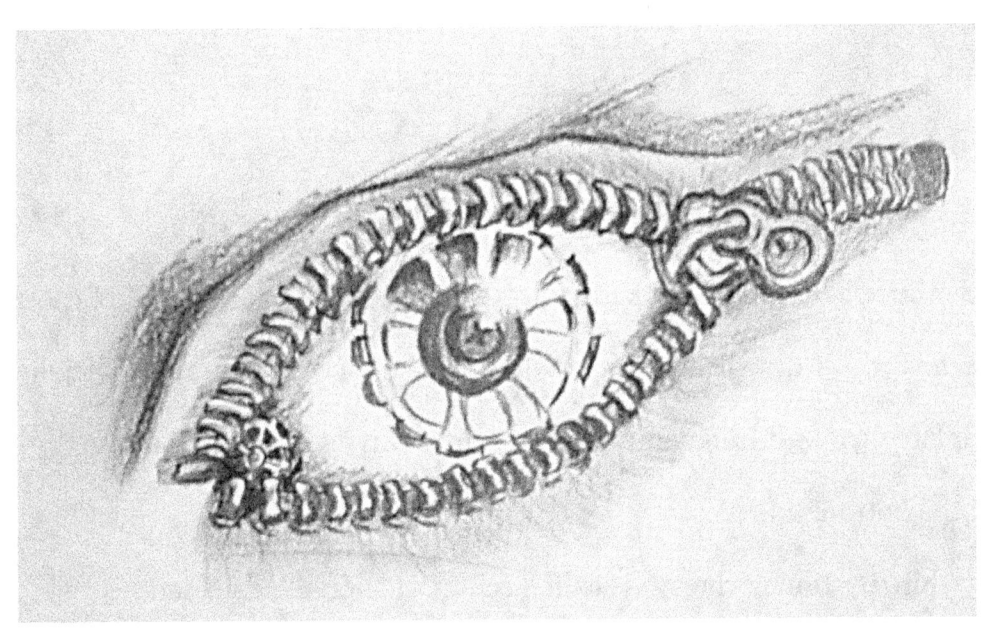

Step 7

Draw the spokes with a dark pencil, while carefully shading the area. A tiny gear has to be drawn at the tear duct. Make sure it is drawn partially. A complete gear will exaggerate the tear duct. Give shading inside the top lid and the bottom lid.

The white portion of the eye is called sclera. It should be shaded neatly.

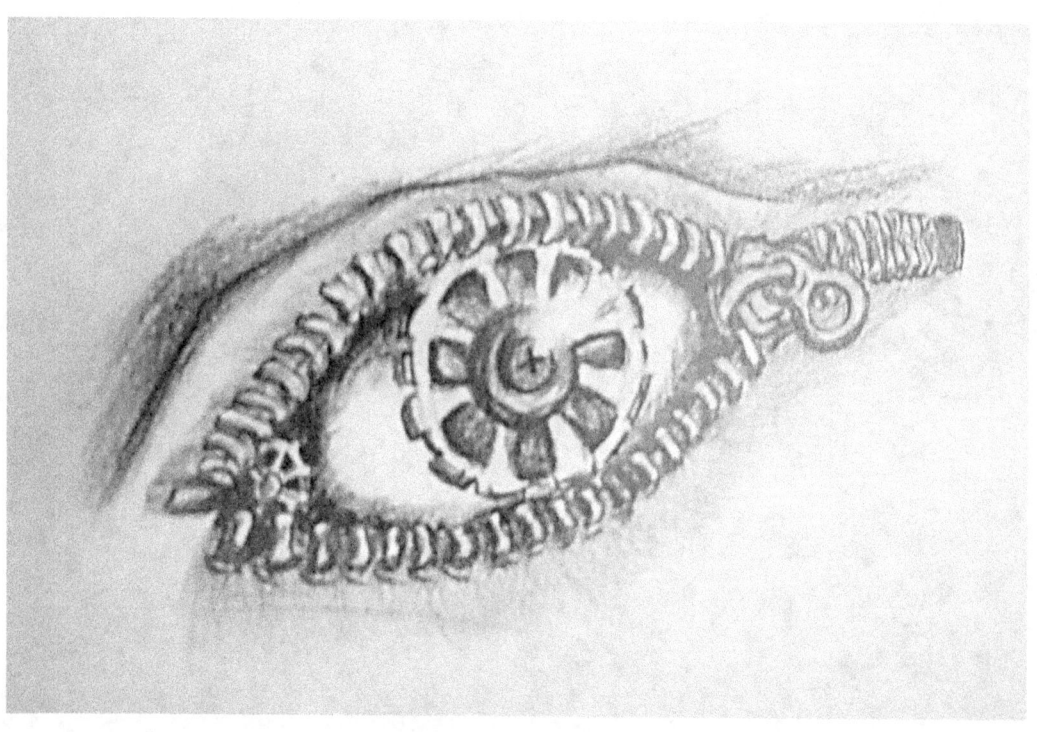

Step 8

Give shading at the "above crease" of the eye. Also give light shading to the area beneath the lower lid.

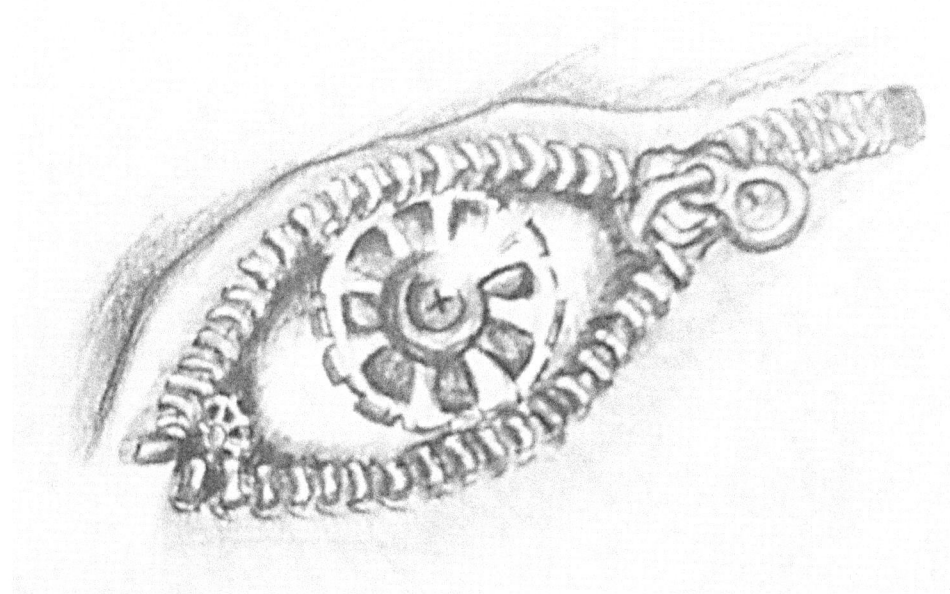

Step 9

Highlight the above crease area with darker pencil shading. But, do not overdo the shading. Give finishing touches to the gears and the zipper teeth.

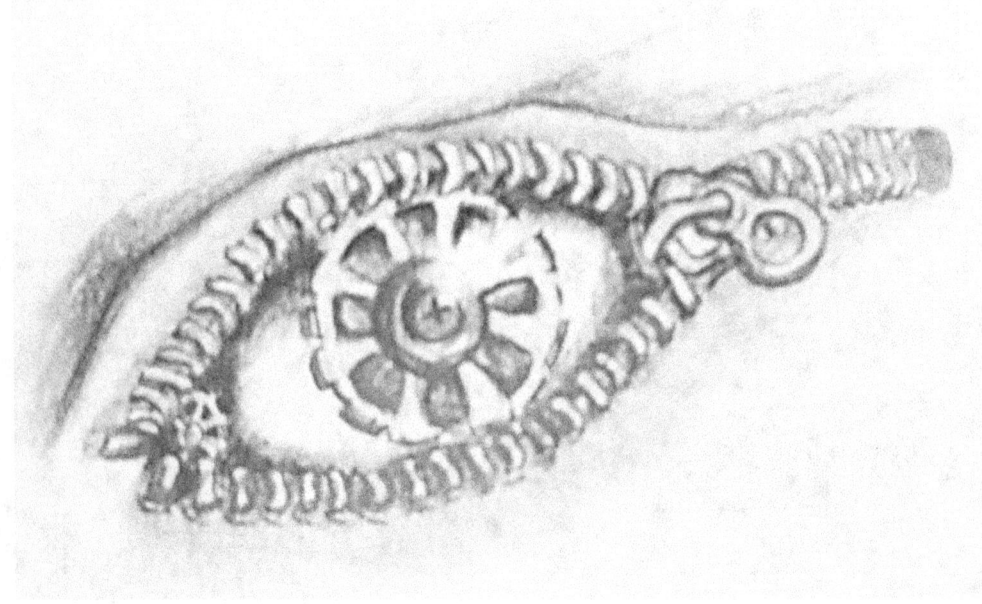

Step 10

Finish the drawing by shading the lower lid area in slightly darker tone. Look for errors, if any and rectify them. Your Steampunk eye is ready.

Try drawing the other eye yourself.

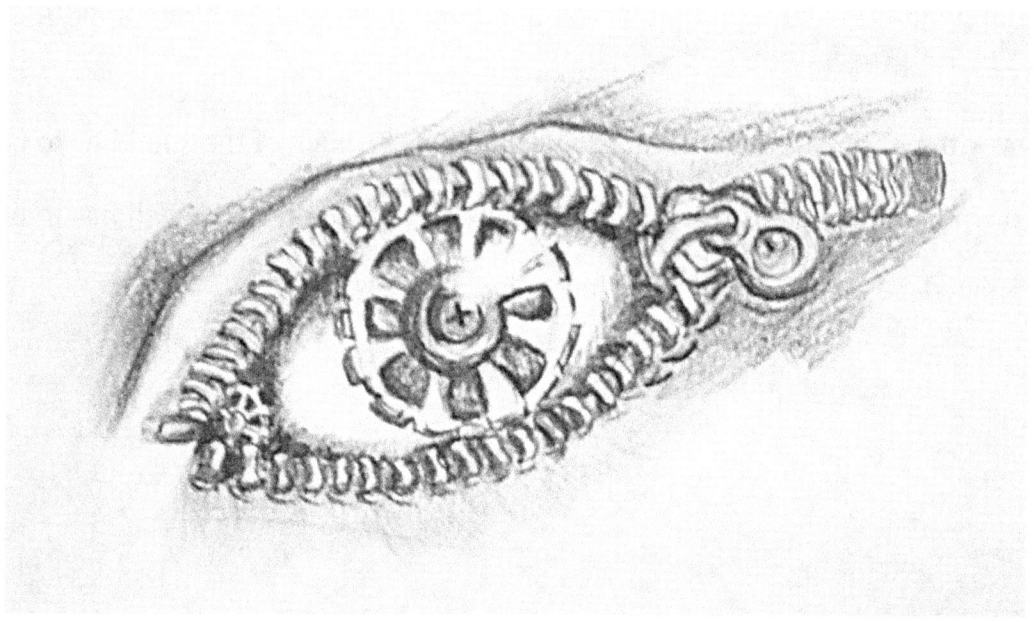

Chapter 3 - A Snail

A snail is a majestic mollusk, which is found on land as well as in sea. They carry a shell on their back, which is used by them to completely retract into it. The shell is like a mobile bed for them. They use this shell for sleeping! Let us try to draw a Steampunk snail.

Step 1

Draw the basic outline of a snail. The shell on the back of the snail has to be drawn with precision. You will find in the later steps that this shell has to be depicted like a baggage in this illustration.

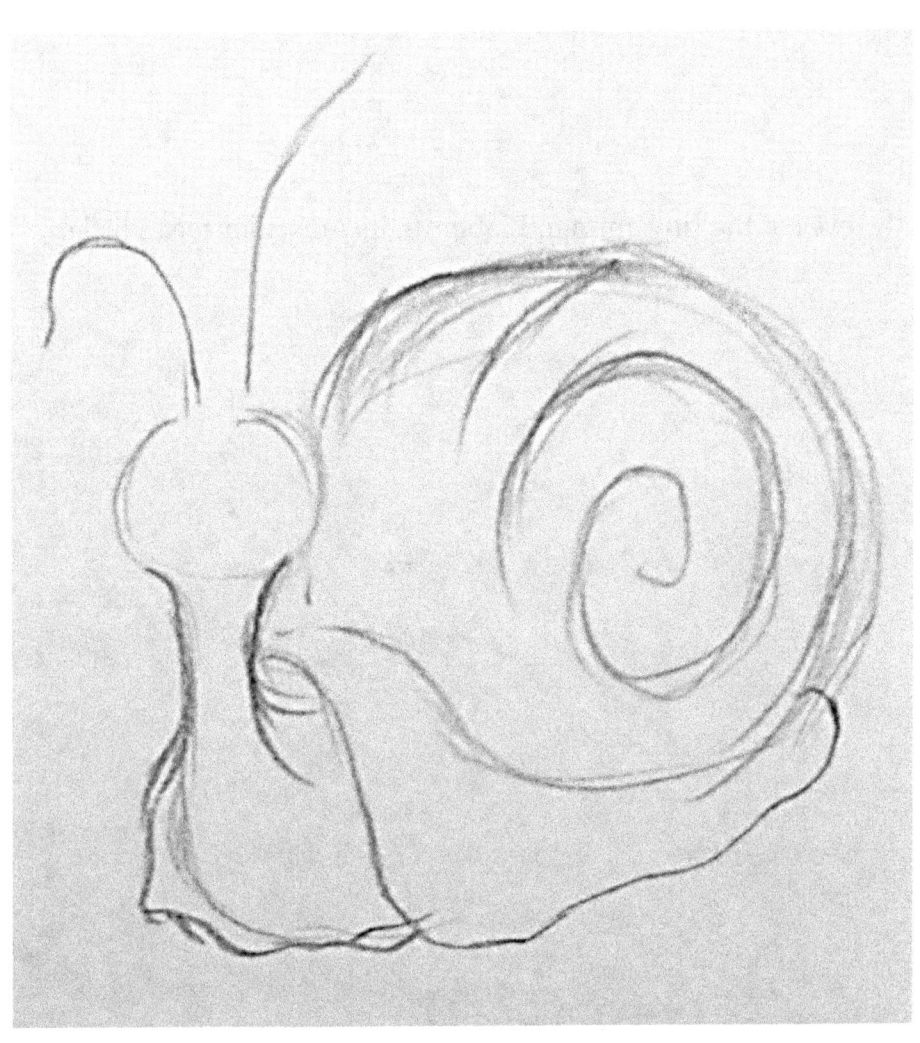

Step 2

Draw the eyes of the tiny animal. Elaborate its muscular feet a little.

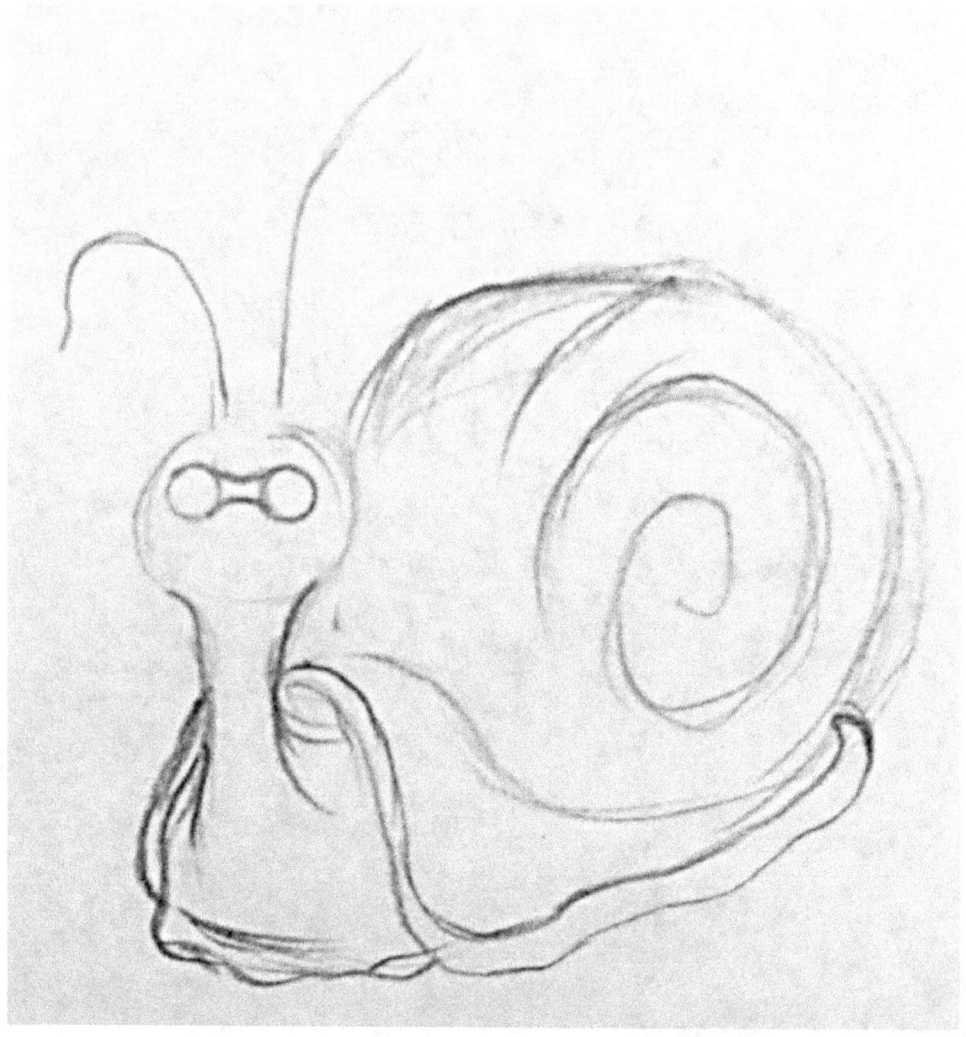

Step 3

Add a collar belt on the neck. And draw the outline of a pair of underwater goggles on the eyes.

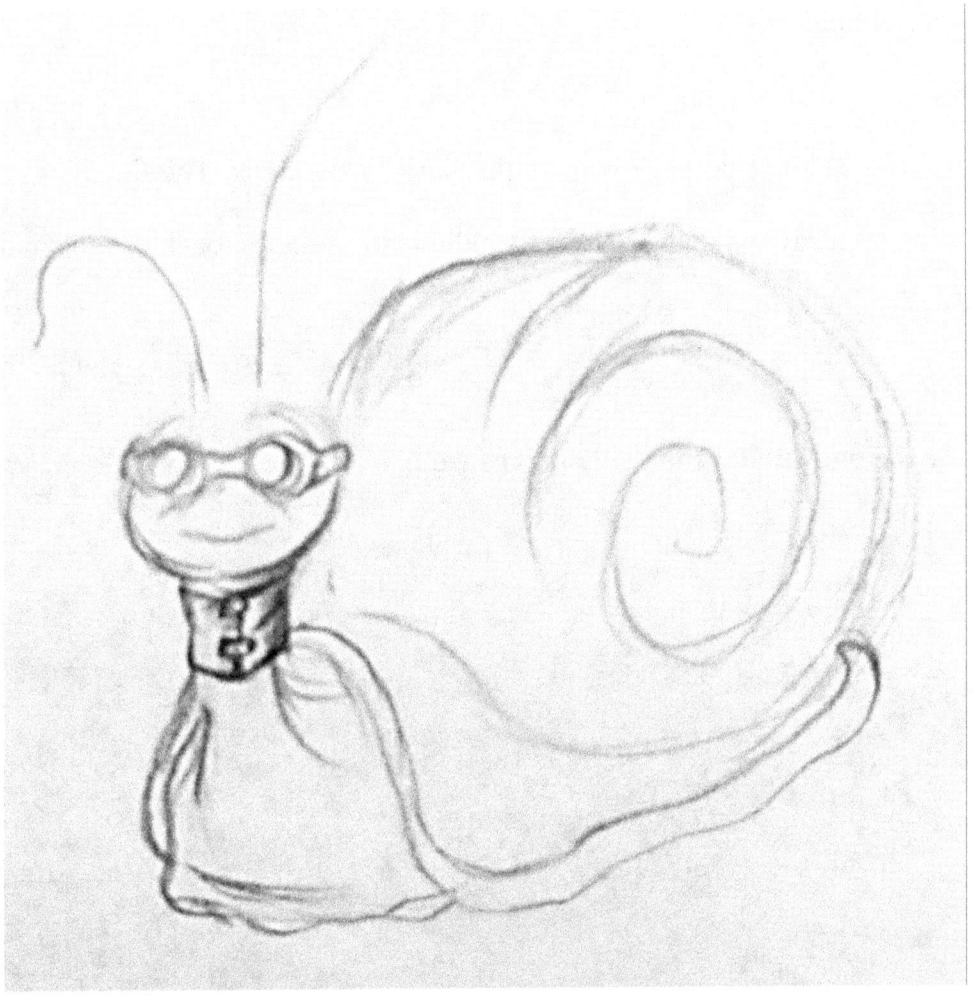

Step 4

Do you know that the antennae of the snails are actually their eyes? Give details to the antennae and the goggles. Draw facial expressions and a lever in the middle of shell to suggest an apparatus which can be moved in a rotational motion.

Notice the saddle that is drawn on the back of the neck. The details of this clothing are drawn like it is leather saddle resting on the back of the snail as it is there on the back of a horse.

Shade the body under the collar belt as well.

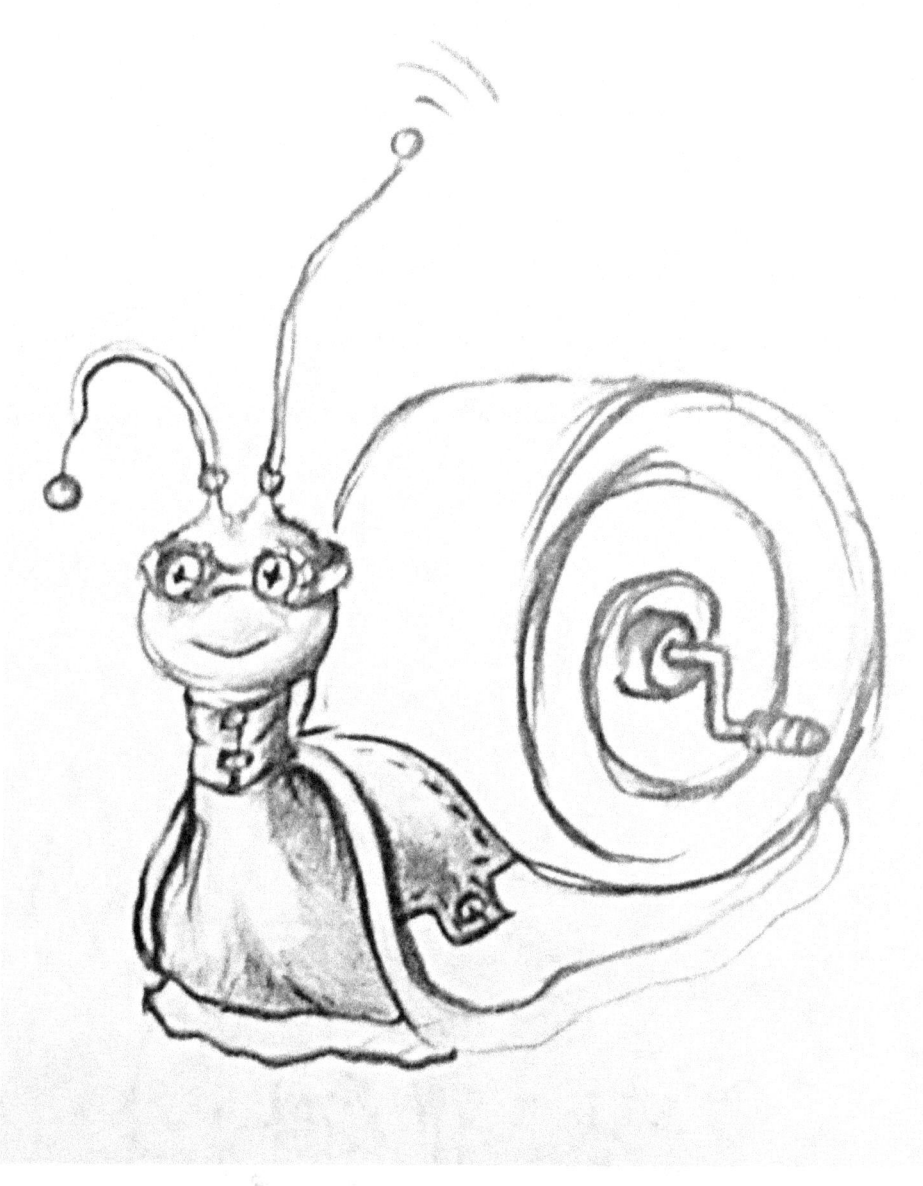

Step 5

Instead of a shell, we have depicted this snail with a baggage on its back. Draw stitches of clothing on the exterior of this baggage. The muscular feet are given details like they are the track of an army tank. Draw the links of this track.

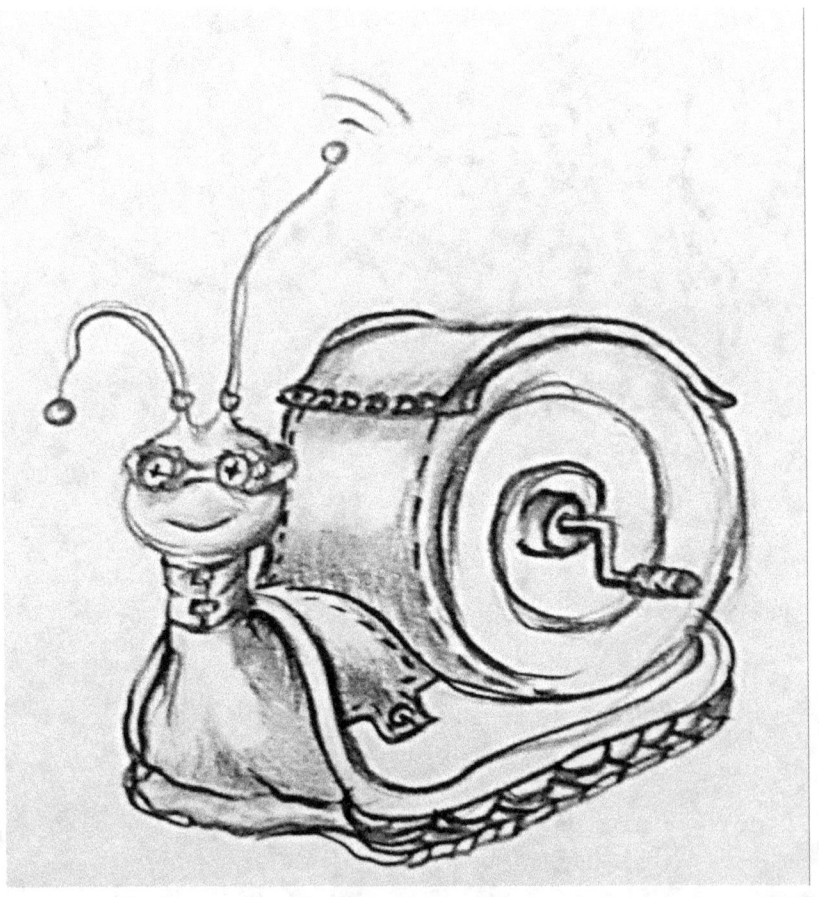

Step 6

Give detailing to the folds of the bedding resting on this tiny animal's back.

Suggest a few buttons or fasteners and the folds of the bedding.

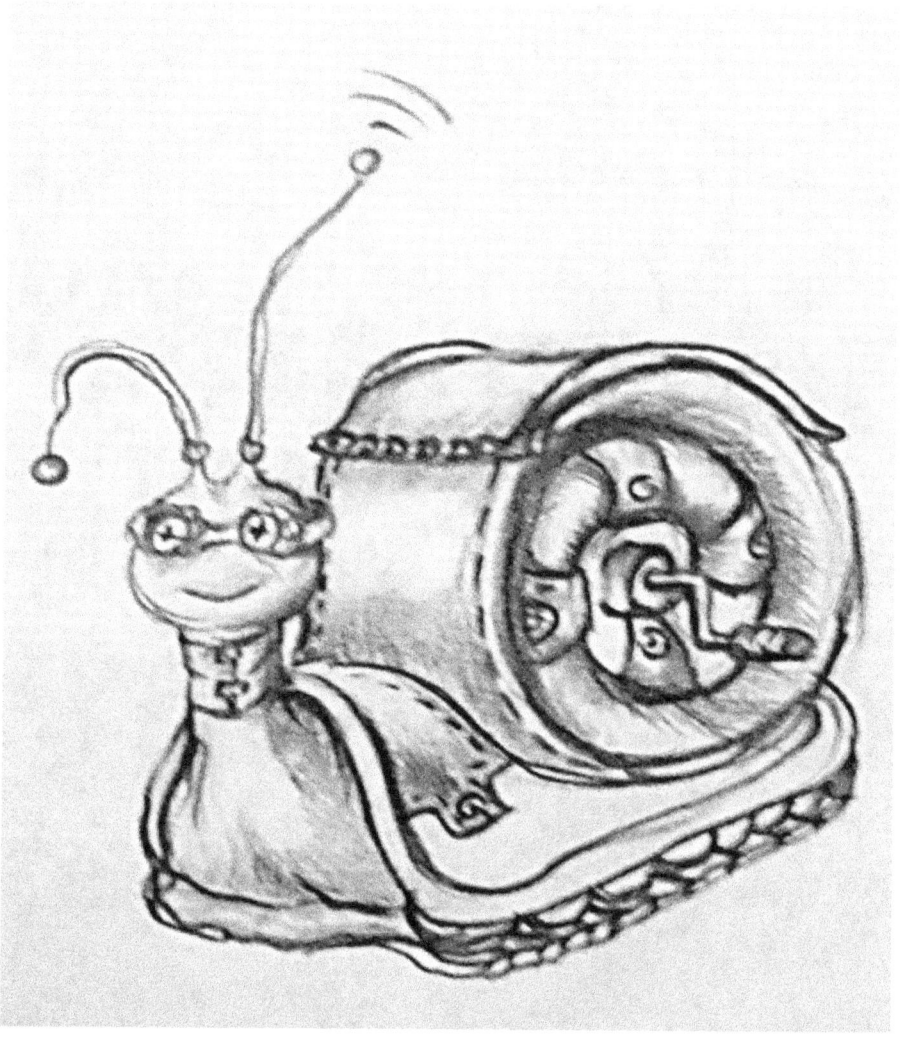

Step 7

Bolden the lines and shading of the snail. Give necessary intricacies required, like the lines suggesting movement of antennae. Some shading has been given beneath the track or feet of the snail to suggest the shadow.

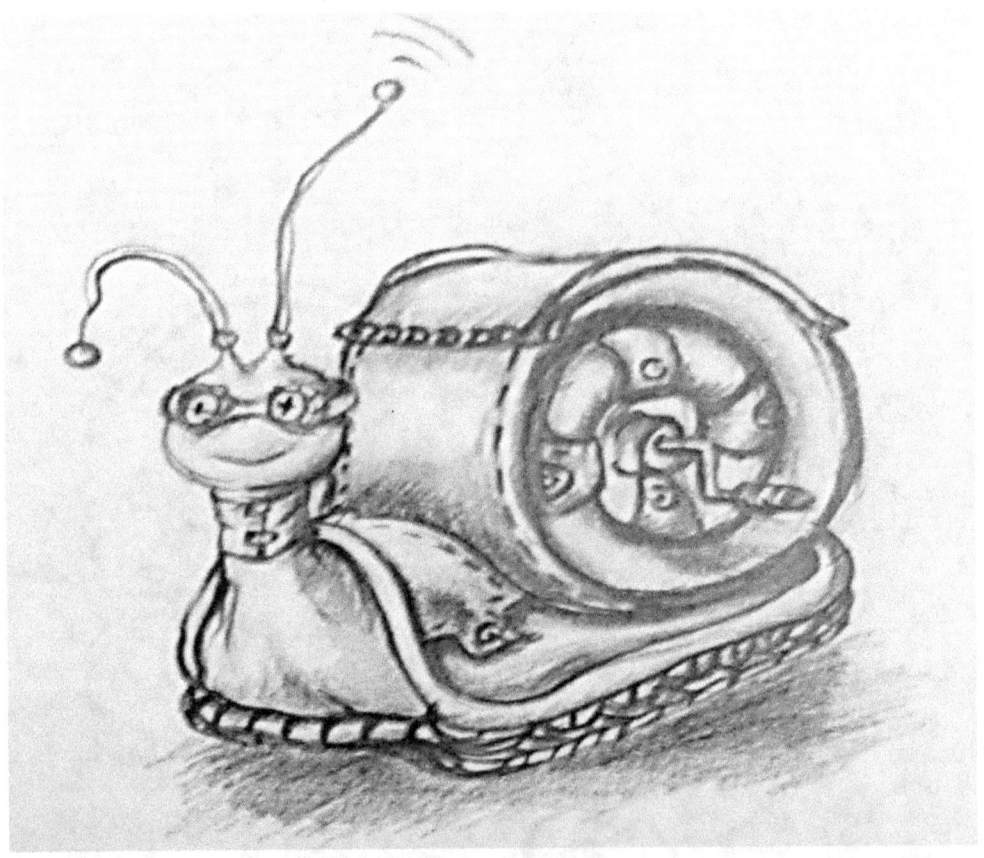

Step 8

In the last step, you just have to suggest necessary highlights that give a realistic look to the illustration. This can be done by giving light and dark shades to various parts of the snail.

Your Steampunk snail is ready. You can try many other Steampunk animals by drawing machine parts of various types in place of their real body parts.

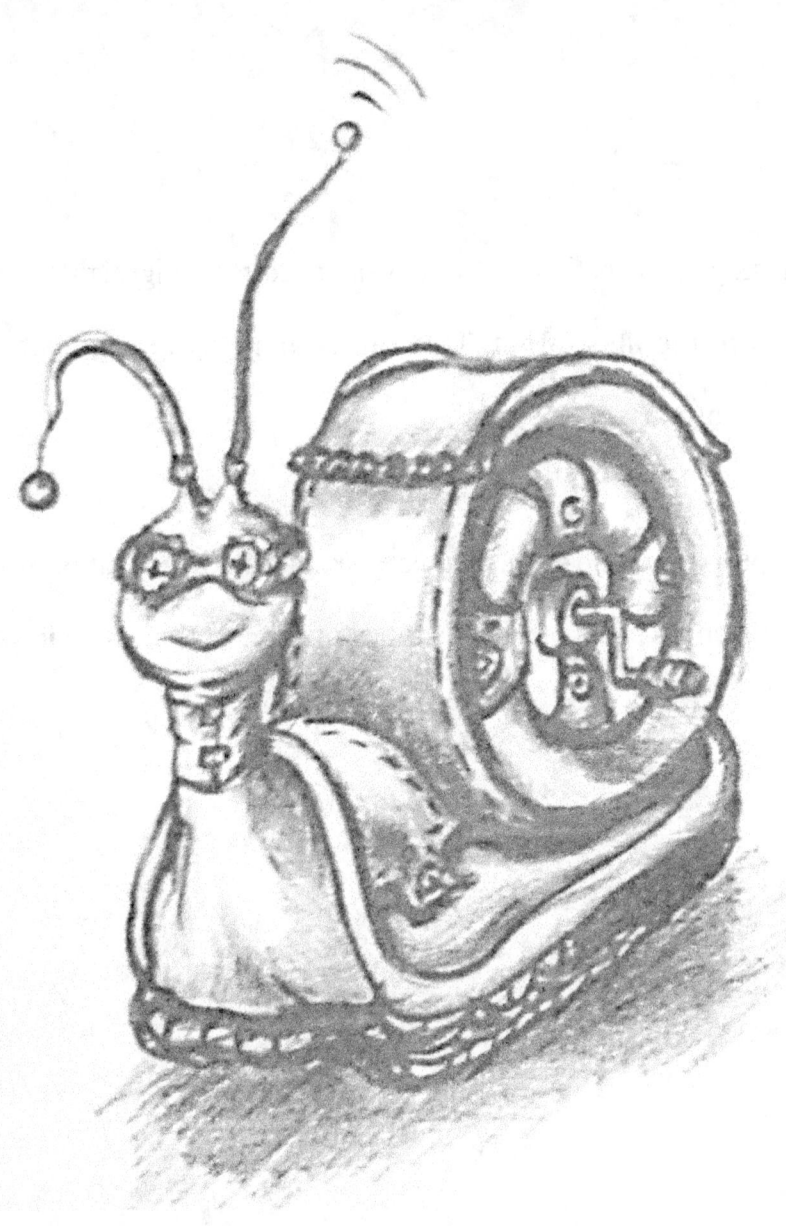

Chapter 4 - A Fist

Step 1

Draw the block outline of a fist.

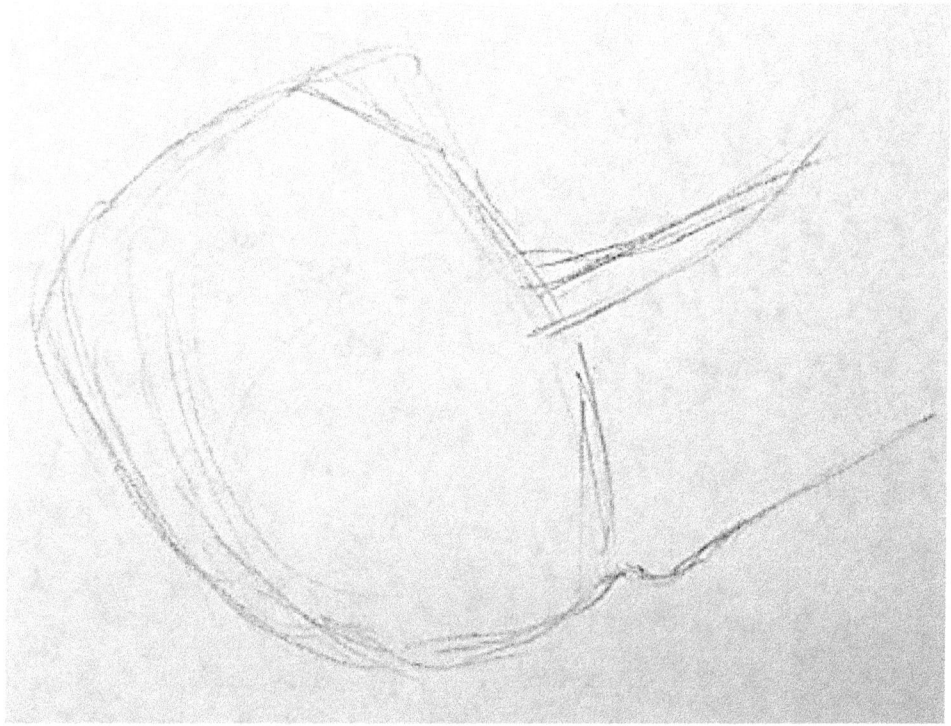

Step 2

We are basically drawing the sketch of a punching fist here. The angle of the wrist and the look of the fist should feel like the hand of a boxer who is about to hit someone.

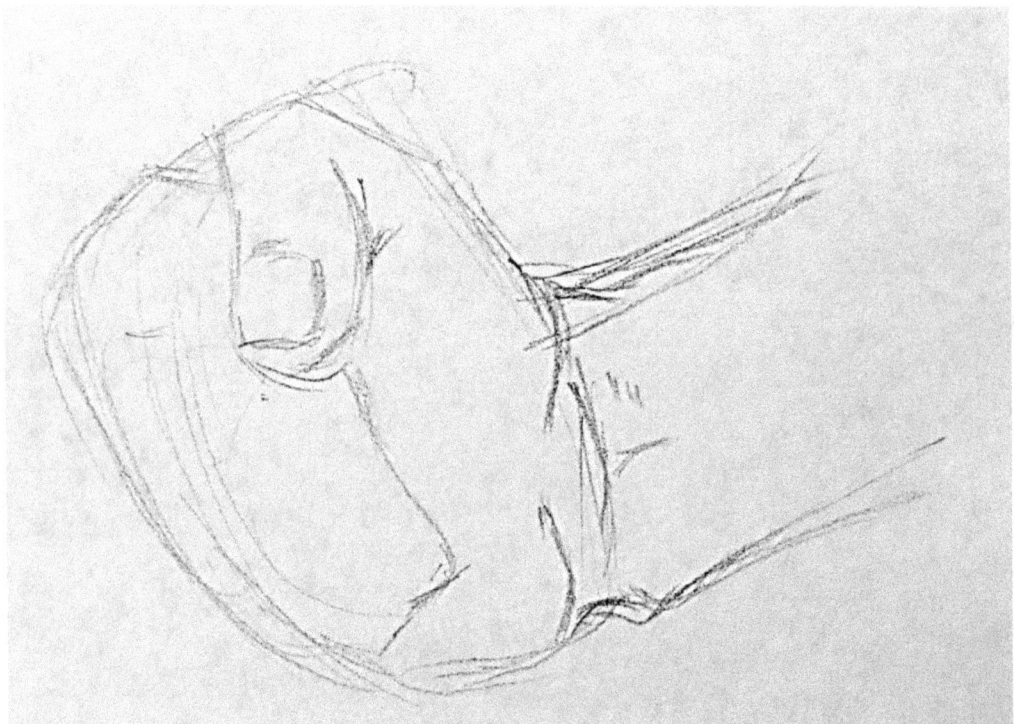

Step 3

Give slight details of the fingers and the thumbnail. The outline of the hand has to be enhanced here. The fold of the hand against the wrist has to be highlighted.

Notice how the skin of the hand folds when you make a fist. Do it yourself with your hand and draw accordingly.

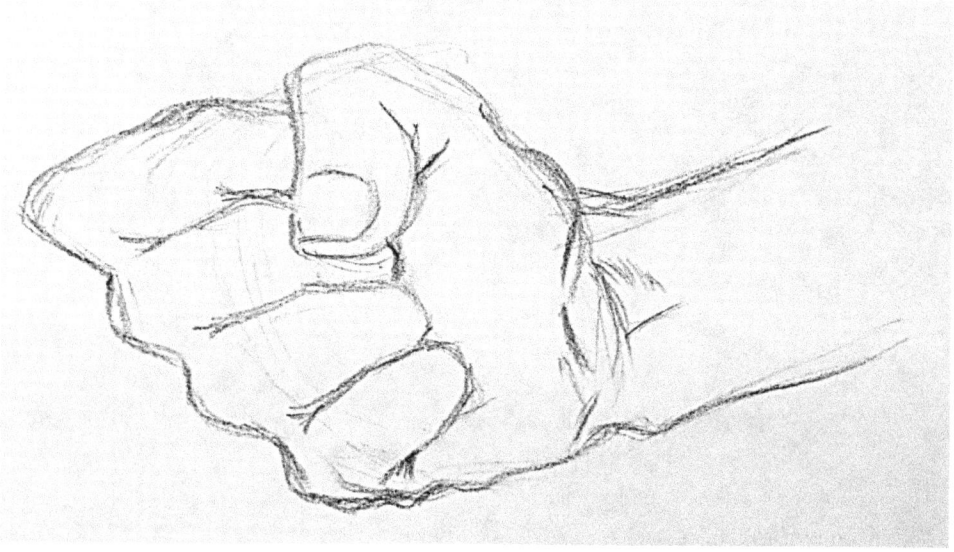

Step 4

Start giving outline of the initial lines of the wrist bands.

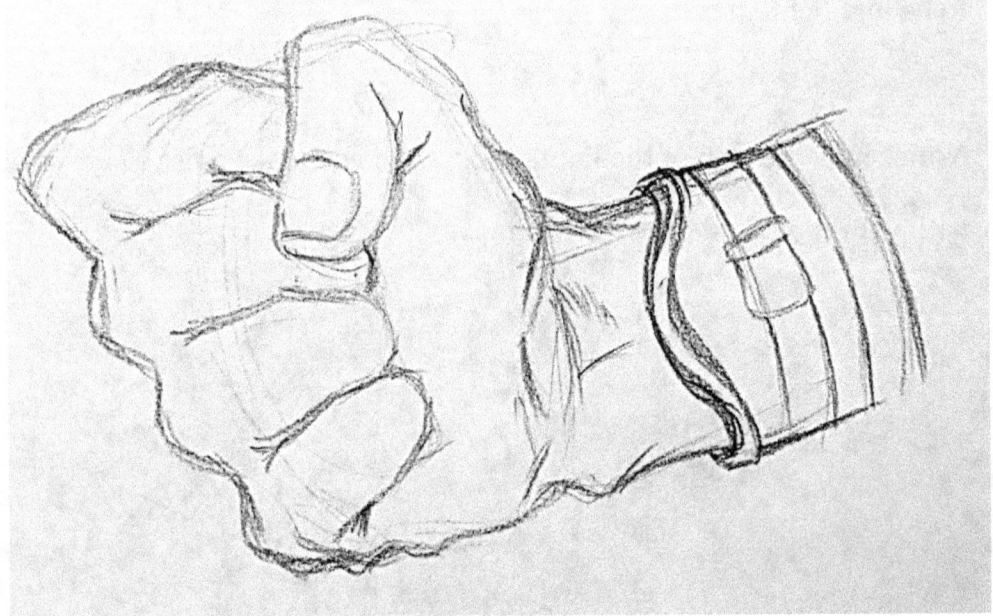

Step 5

Draw the buckles of the wrist bands on the inside of the wrist. Give attention to the holes of the bands. They have been drawn partly in circle. The shading is also done partly. This gives a 3D touch to the belt of the bands.

Draw a gear with spikes and spokes. Add a simple wrist band without a buckle near the gear.

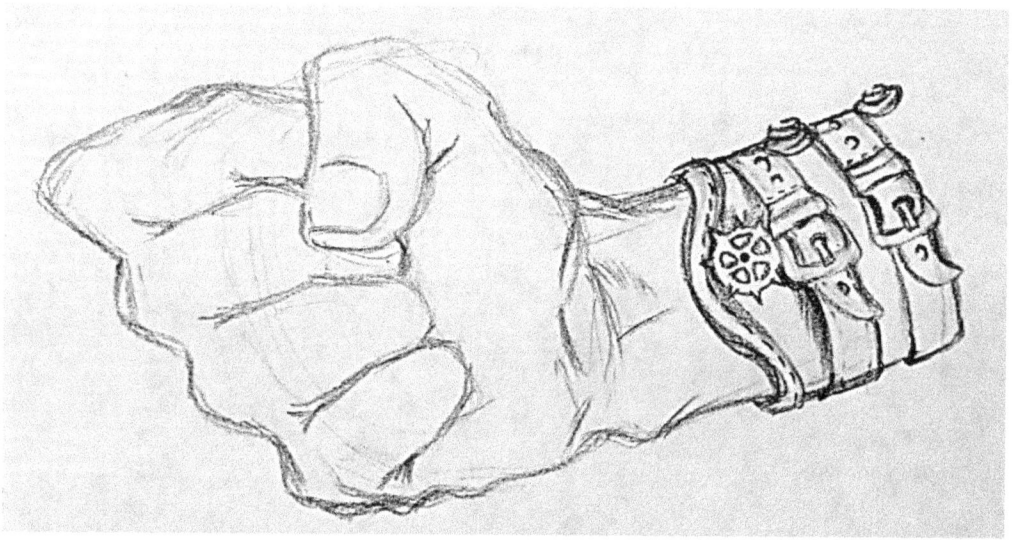

Step 6

Add two fastener-like buttons near the wrist bands.

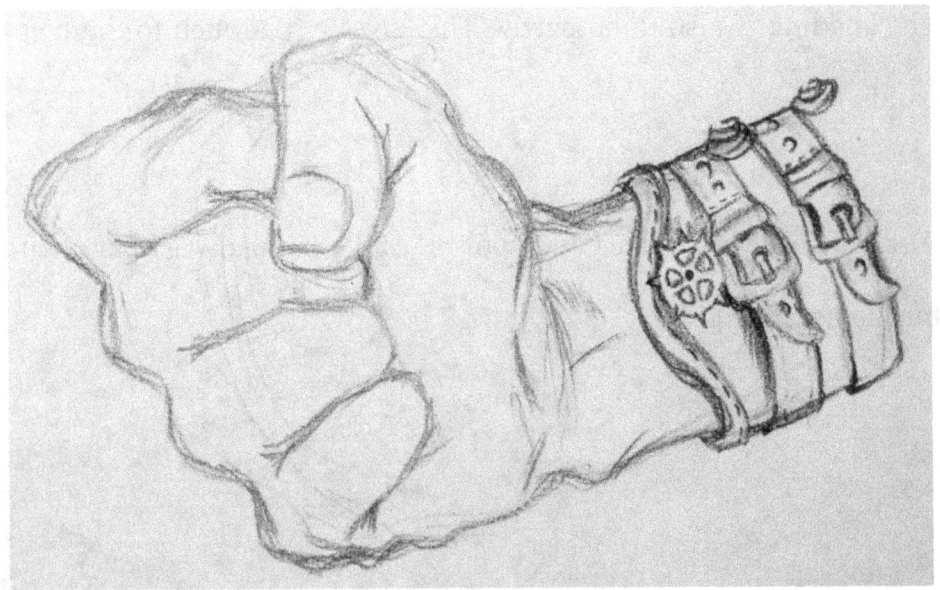

Step 7

Shade the skin of the forearm between the wrist bands. Give a little detail to the nerves at the wrist.

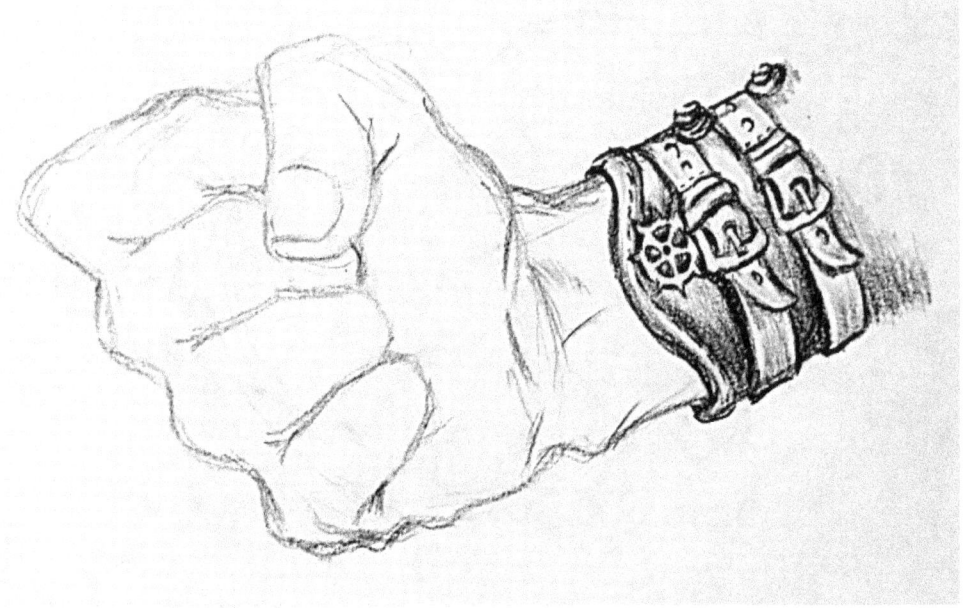

Step 8

Start making the outline of knuckle guards. They should cover just the knuckles, not the complete fingers.

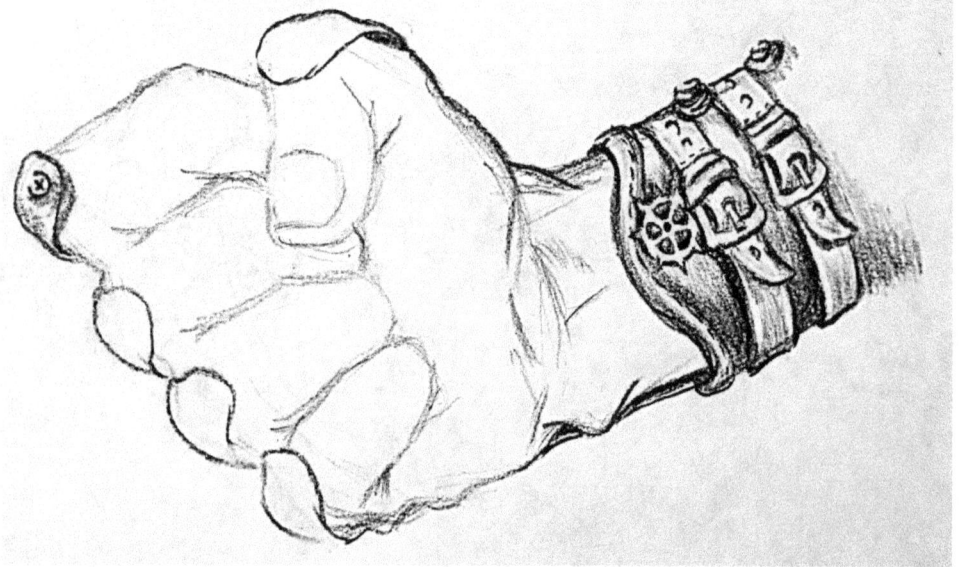

Step 9

The knuckle guards are given details in this step. Notice the "+" sign on the guards. They are made as if you can fasten the knuckle guards with a screwdriver and then unfasten them at your will.

This is depicted as the hand of a strong Steampunk boxer.

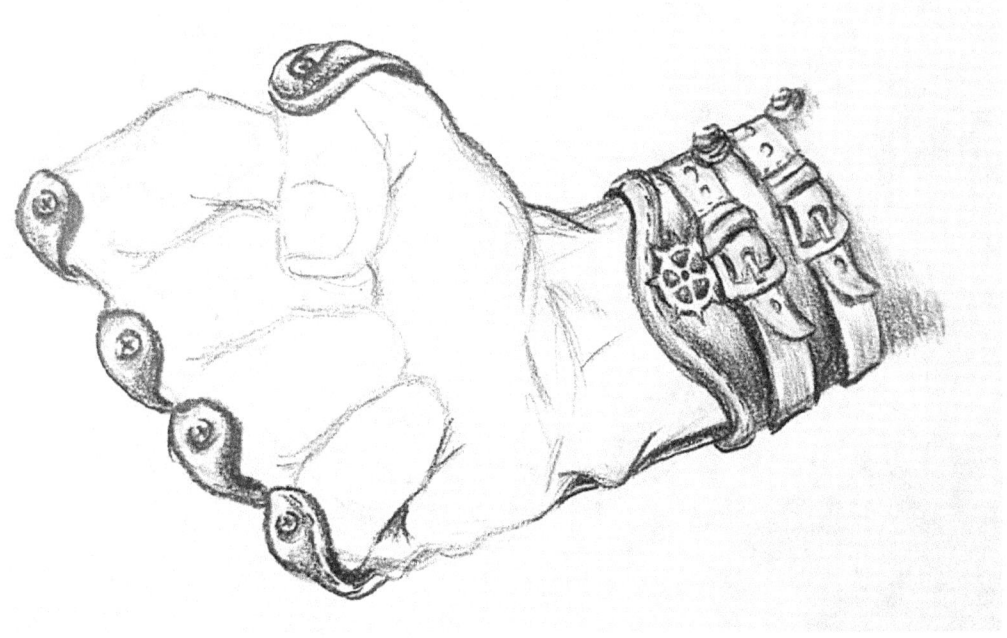

Step 10

Give shading to the fingers and the thumbnail. Notice the shadow that is falling on the palm because of the fingers that are folded inside. Also, notice the bump on the side of the wrist. Fine lines are added to suggest the muscles of the forearm.

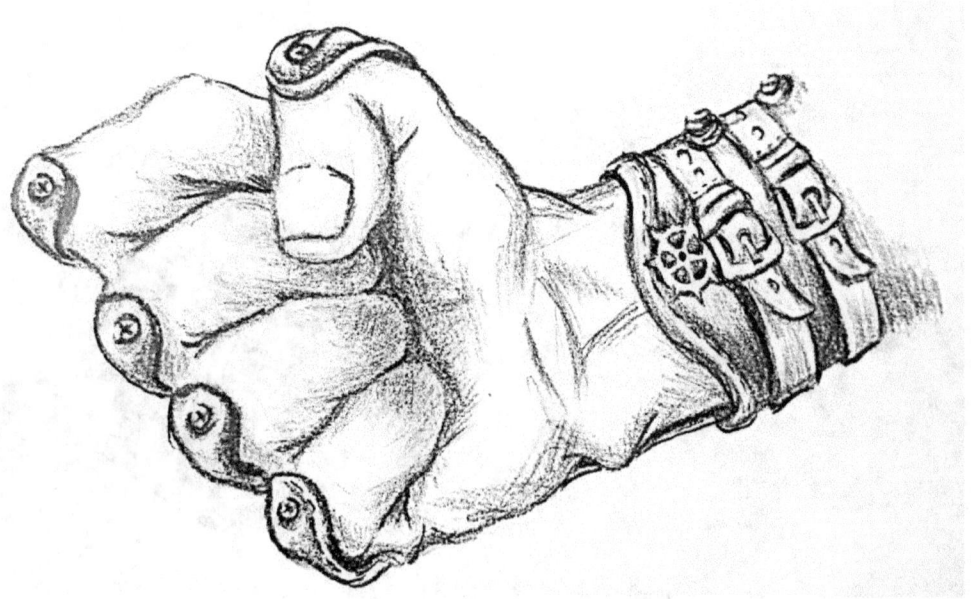

Step 11

Draw the finest details of the inner folds of the knuckles in the fingers. The hand should get the look of a tightened fist. This can be achieved by adding the wrinkles that are caused when someone folds their fingers tightly.

Finish by darkening the shading wherever required. You may give the shining texture to the skin of the palm by erasing the shading in a small area.

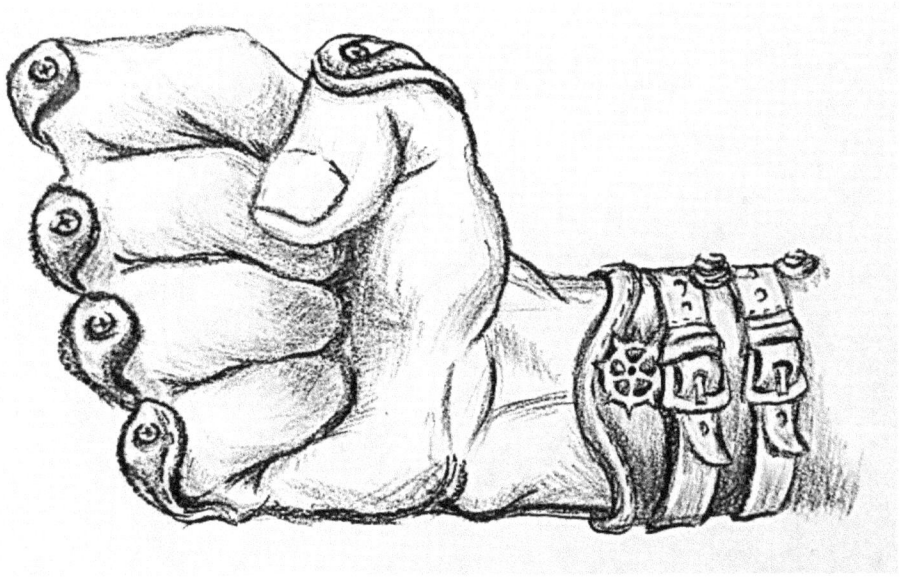

Chapter 5 - -A Fish

Millions of fishes are there in the oceans and our aquariums as well. It is one of the favorite subjects of professional artists and amateurs alike. They can be drawn in any shape and size. They are a popular subject because of the flexibility of design they offer in drawing and painting. Especially the eyes of the fishes are amazing to draw.

Step 1

Draw the basic outline of a fish with an elaborate tail and an elliptical eye.

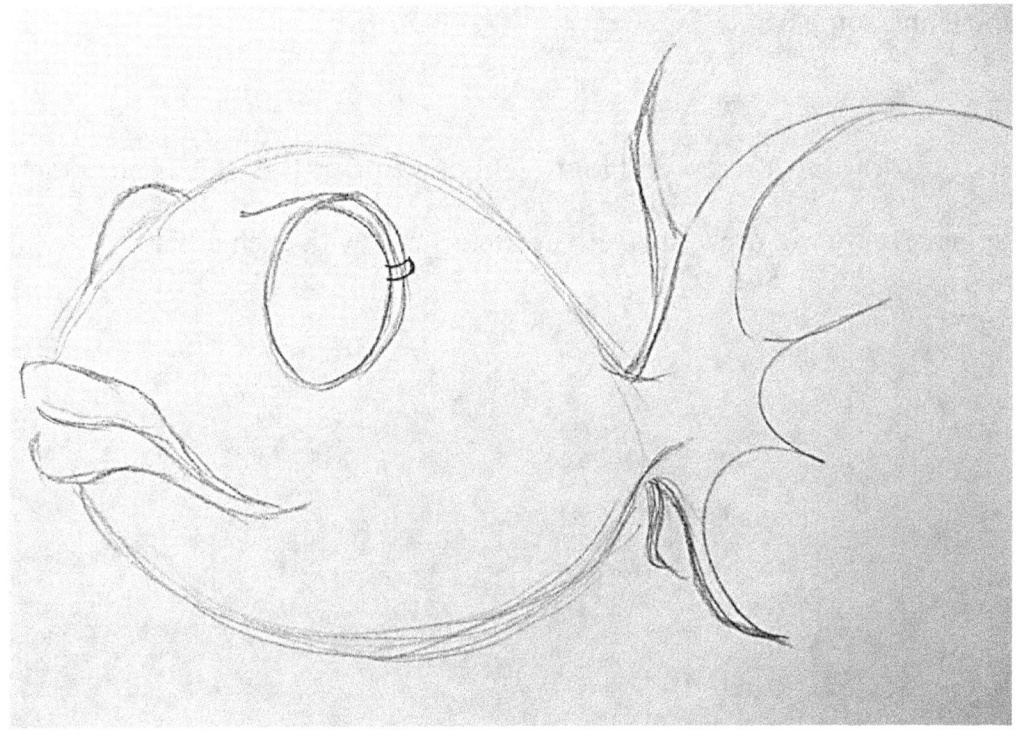

Step 2

When we finish the eye, we want to achieve the effect of an eye fastened with a nail and some belts.

Start by drawing a screw and four teeth of a zipper. But, this is not exactly a zipper. So, we will draw the teeth at some space with each other.

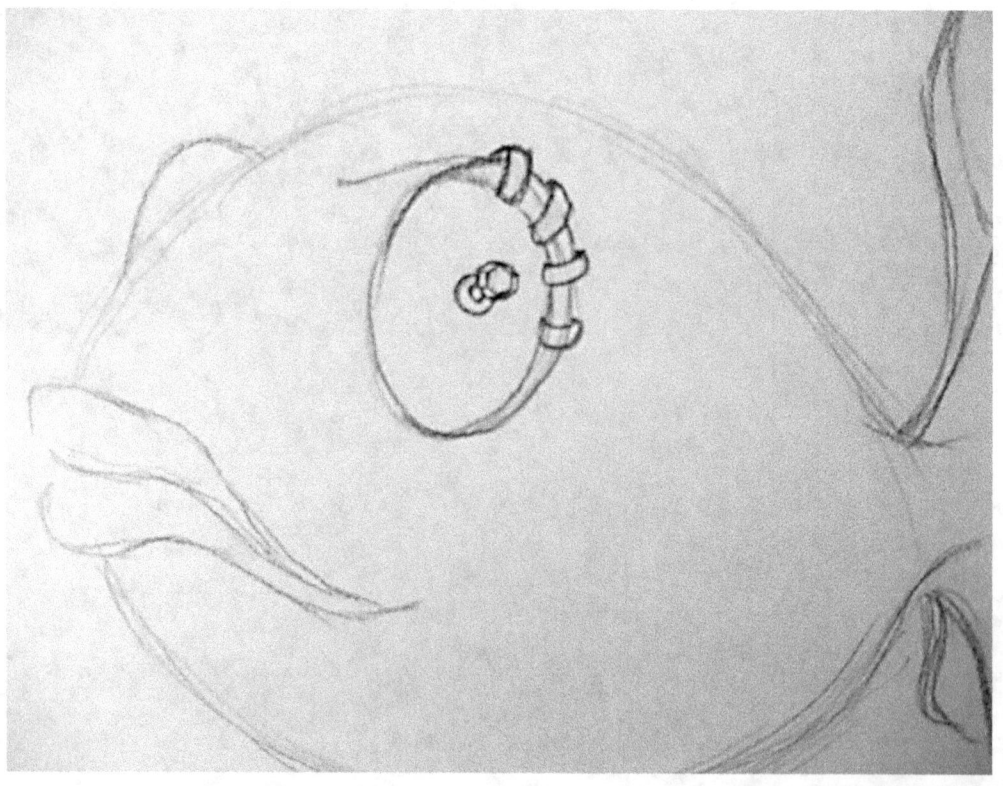

Step 3

Draw some belts on the eye ball, starting from the outer circle of the eye ball and converging at the central screw. Draw one more concentric circle under the belts. This inner circle will be made like a gear in the next step.

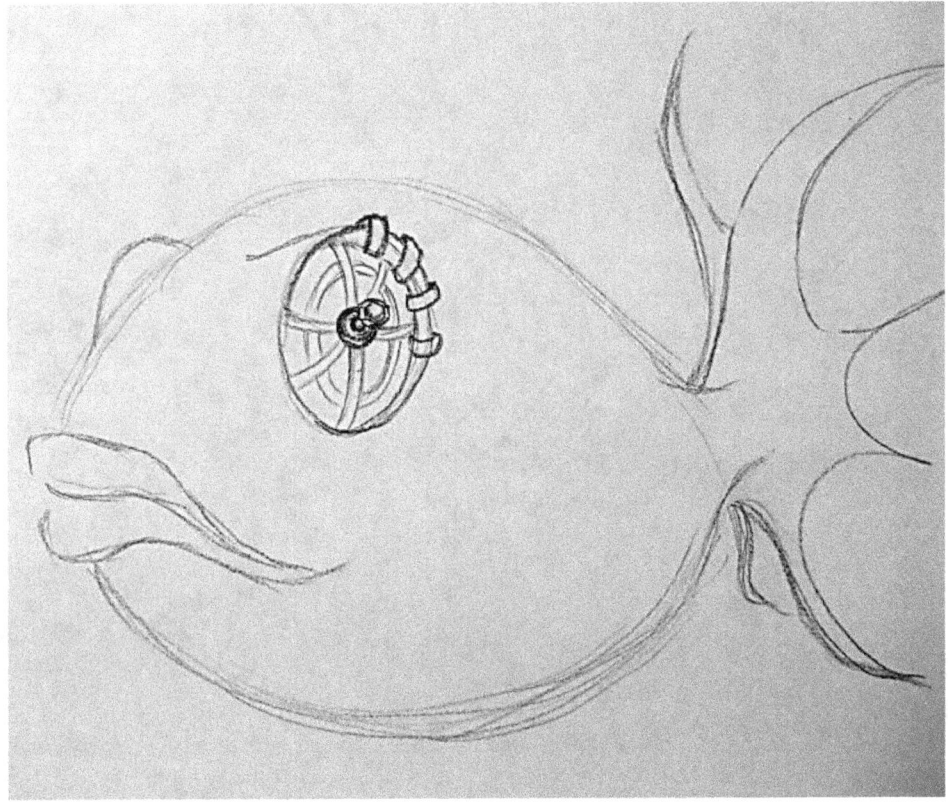

Step 4

Draw the teeth of the gear and highlight the belts lying over the eye ball. Darken the area inside the gear and outside its teeth. Highlight the teeth of the zipper as well.

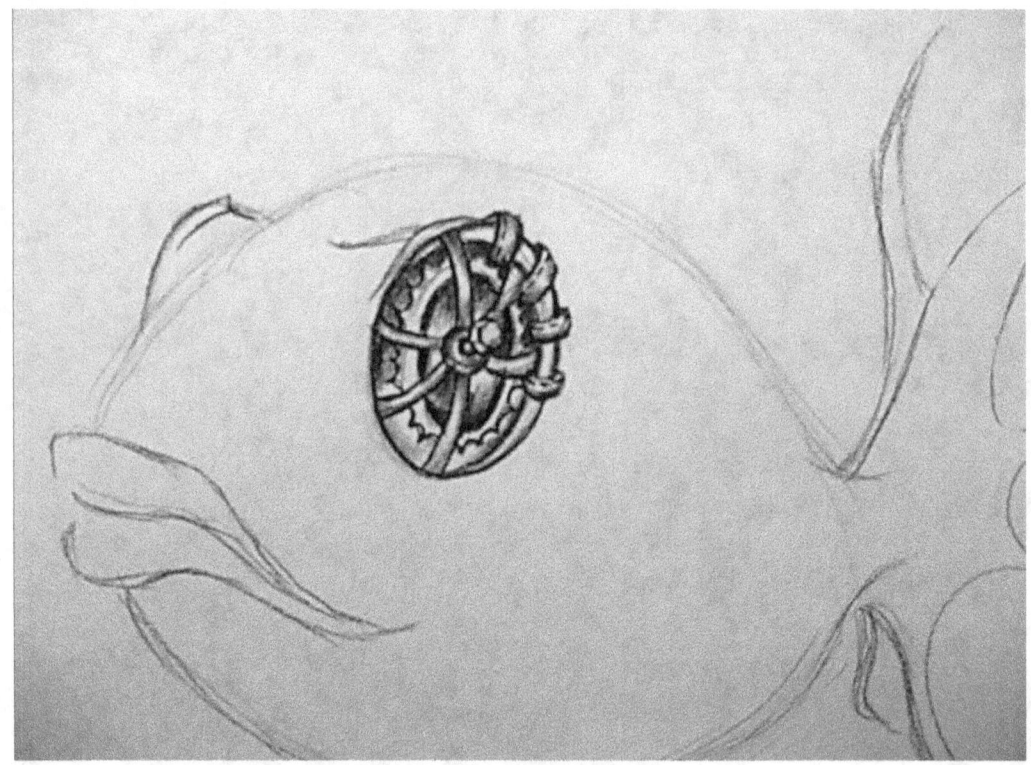

Step 5

Highlight the dorsal fin over the head of the fish. Here, we are making it more like a crown over its head. Draw some stitches on it and give shading to the folds and creases of the fin.

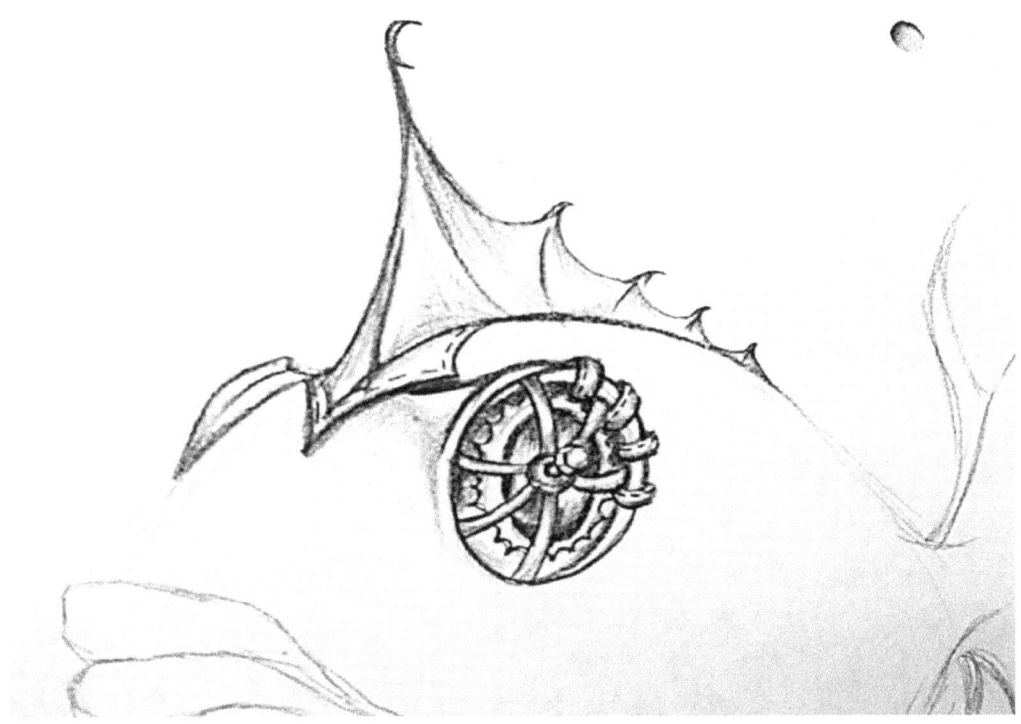

Step 7

Make two fasteners on the body, one near the lips and one slightly away from the eye. Connect them with two thin shafts. Also, draw more circles for making gears afterwards.

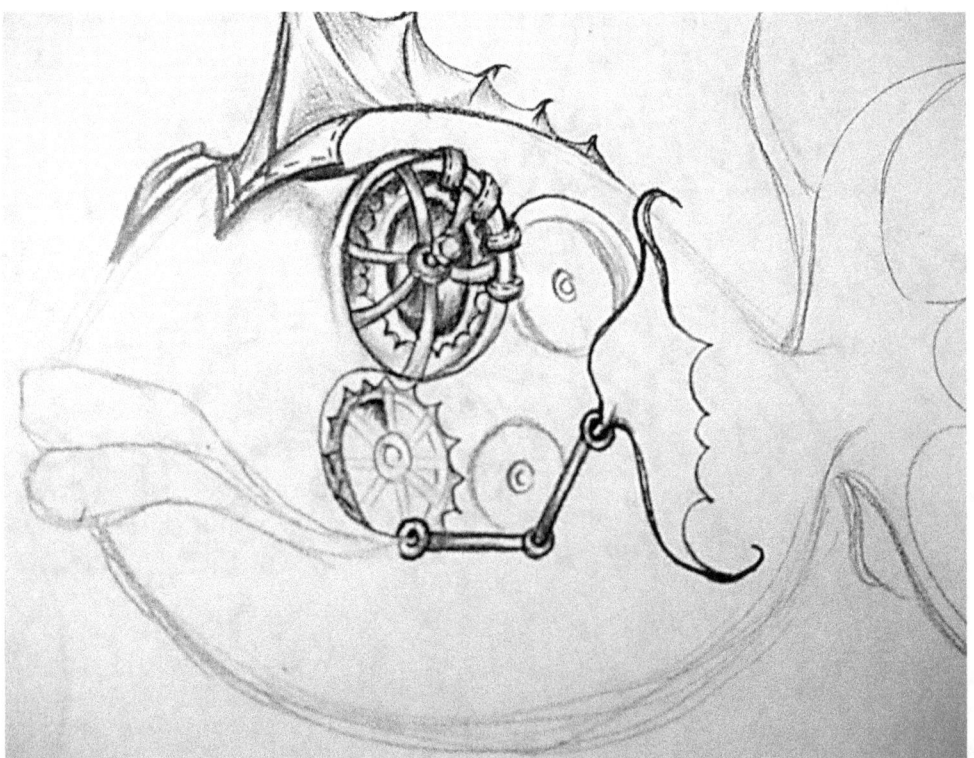

Step 8

Give a brief outline of a saddle type embellishment on the lower portion of the fish, coming from underneath the lips.

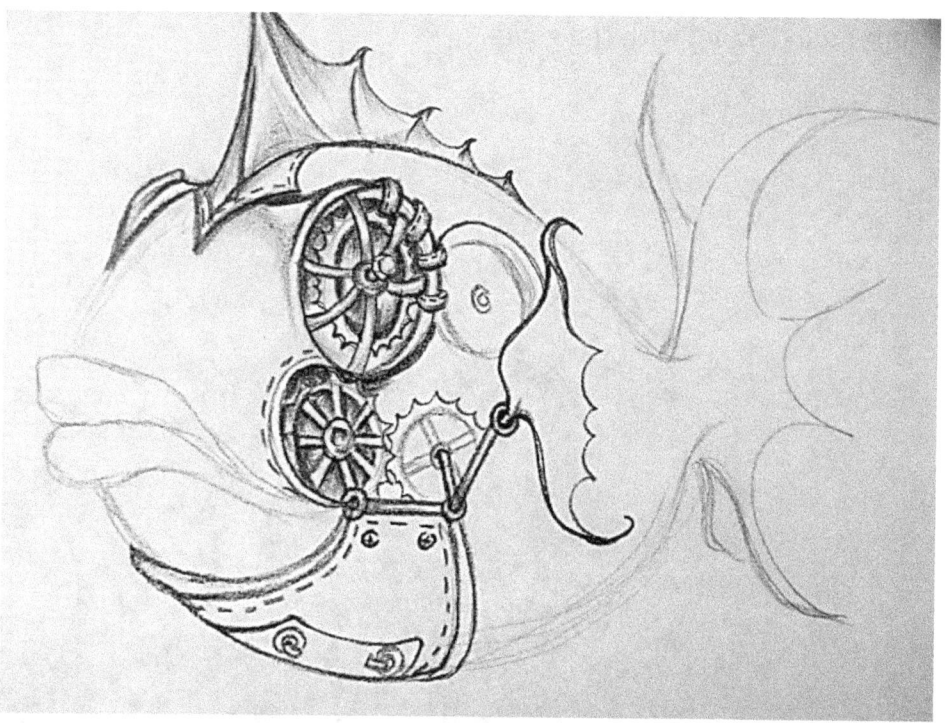

Step 9

Enhance the saddle and give details to the smaller gears. The gears here look like a combination of wheels and gears. Thus, the spokes resemble those of wheels, but the outer teeth resemble those of gears. Notice a fin that is added along with the gears.

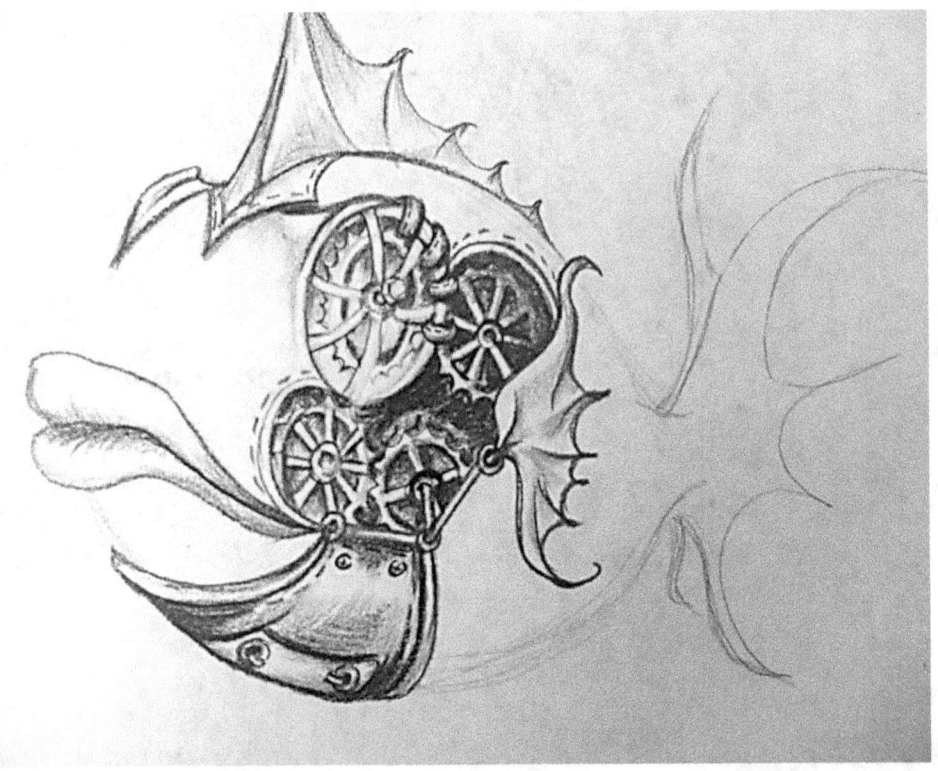

Step 10

Give shading near the lips and the lower body.

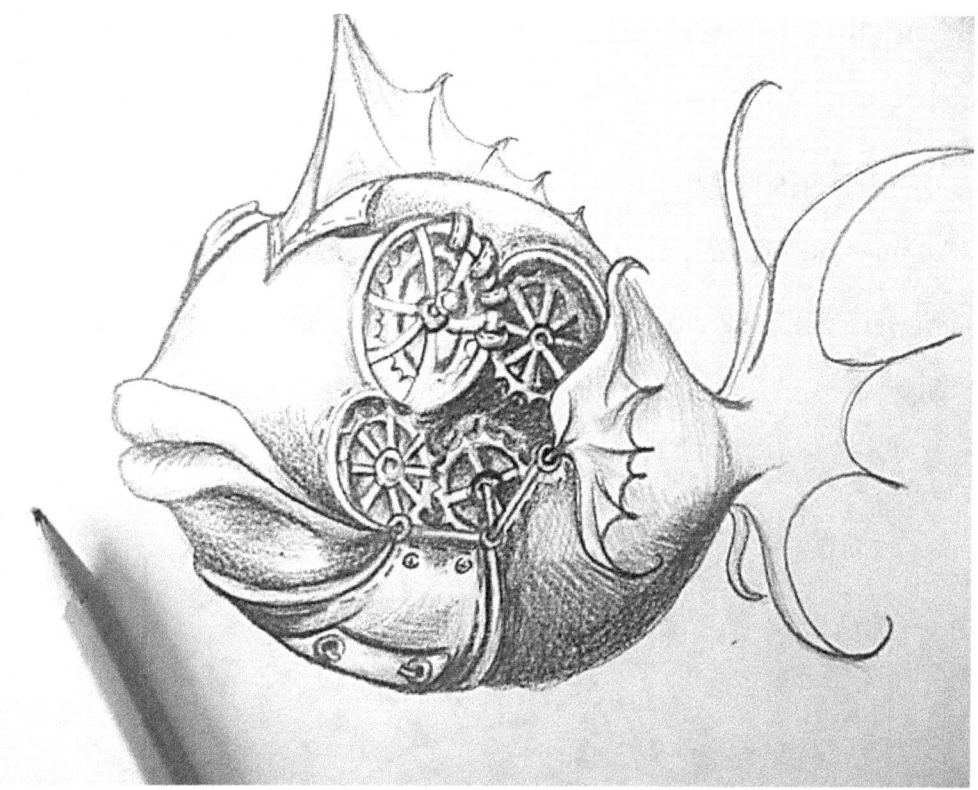

Step 11

Shade the tail and the rear body. Give finishing touches to the fish by darkening and lightening the shading wherever required. Also, briefly touch the intricate details like stitching marks and corners of the fins etc.

When you complete this Steampunk fish, it looks like an automated submarine. At first sight, it would appear like a sea-fish, but when the viewers will look closely, it would look like a mechanized creature of the sea.

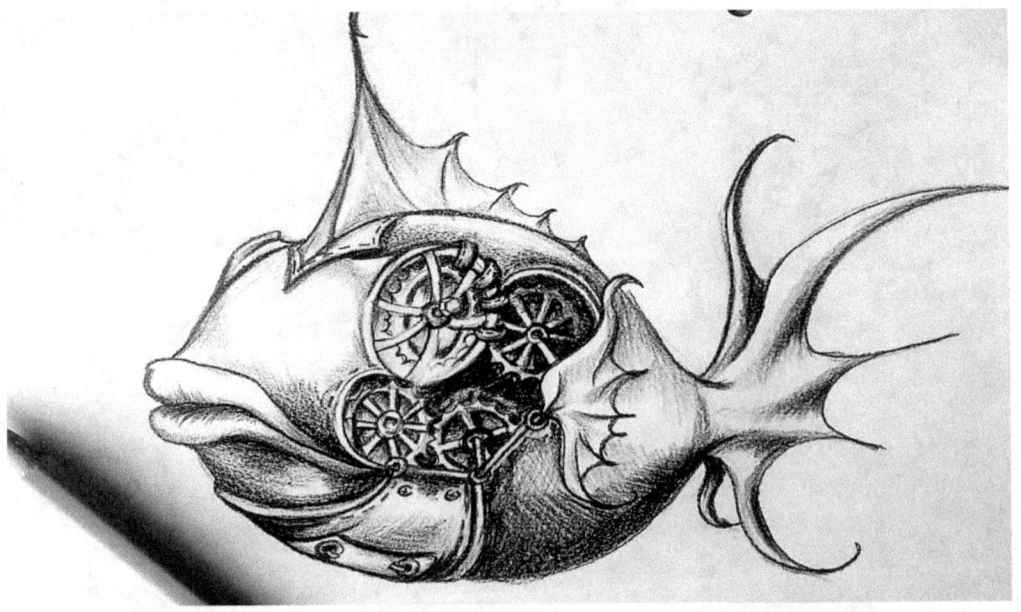

Chapter 6 - A Book with a Pen

For the intellectual artist minds, we have a treat. A Steampunk book along with a pen is illustrated here. You might have drawn many books and pens during your practice sessions. They are easy to draw and provide enormous scope for artistic exploration. The different angles and perspectives of the book as well as the pen allow a lot of scope for shading and drawing.

Let us start with drawing a Steampunk book.

Step 1

Draw the outline of the book with an attached pen holder on its spine. Just give a slight suggestion of a pen. We will give details to the pen in the next step.

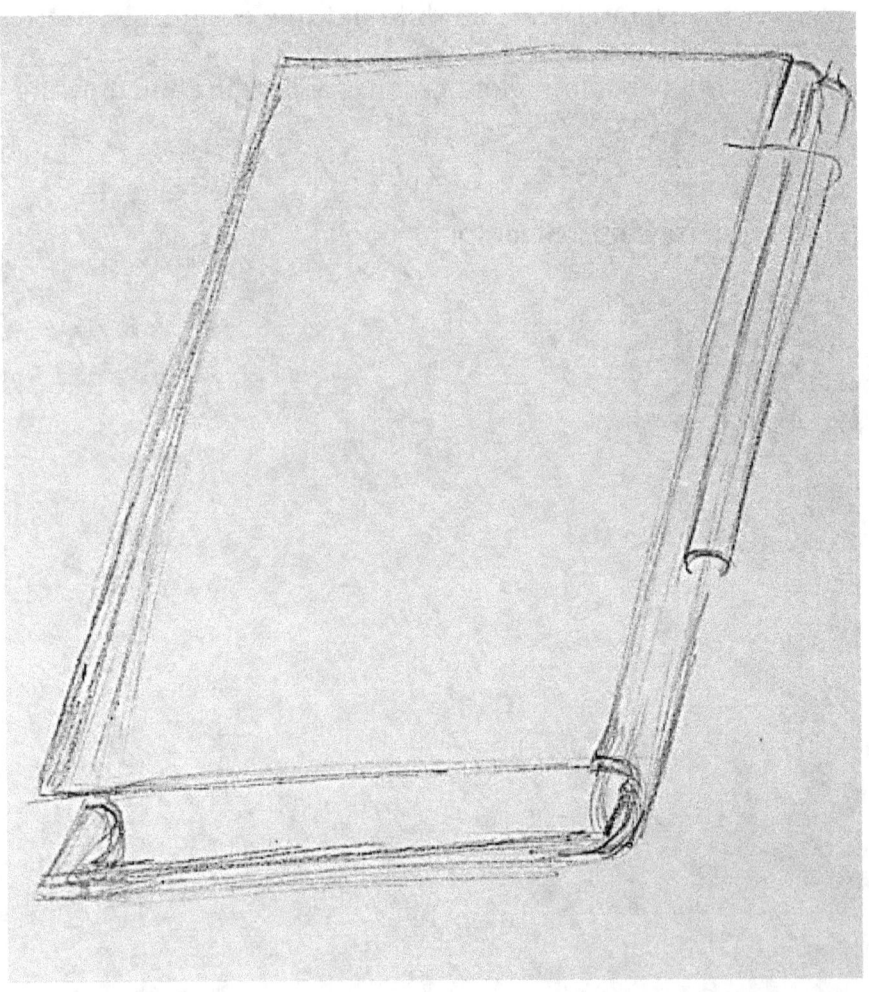

Step 2

Give a detailed outline to the pen with a ball on the top as the push buttons are there in the modern clicking pens. Draw the nib and give detailing to the front part of the pen. Briefly outline the pen holder as well.

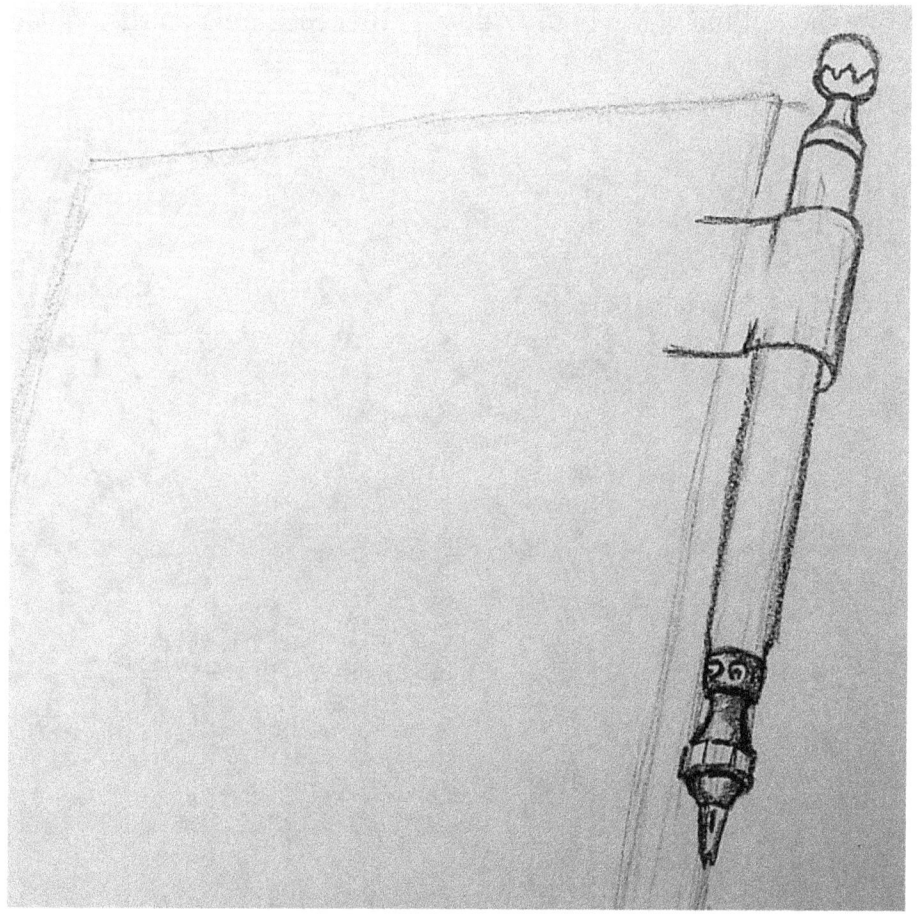

Step 3

Give shading to the body of the pen. Highlight the outline as well. Draw stitches on the pen holder. Notice the nails that are inserted on the pen holder. Such intricate details add life to the drawings. Do not forget to draw them.

Refine the outline of the book. Add an inner rectangle on the book cover.

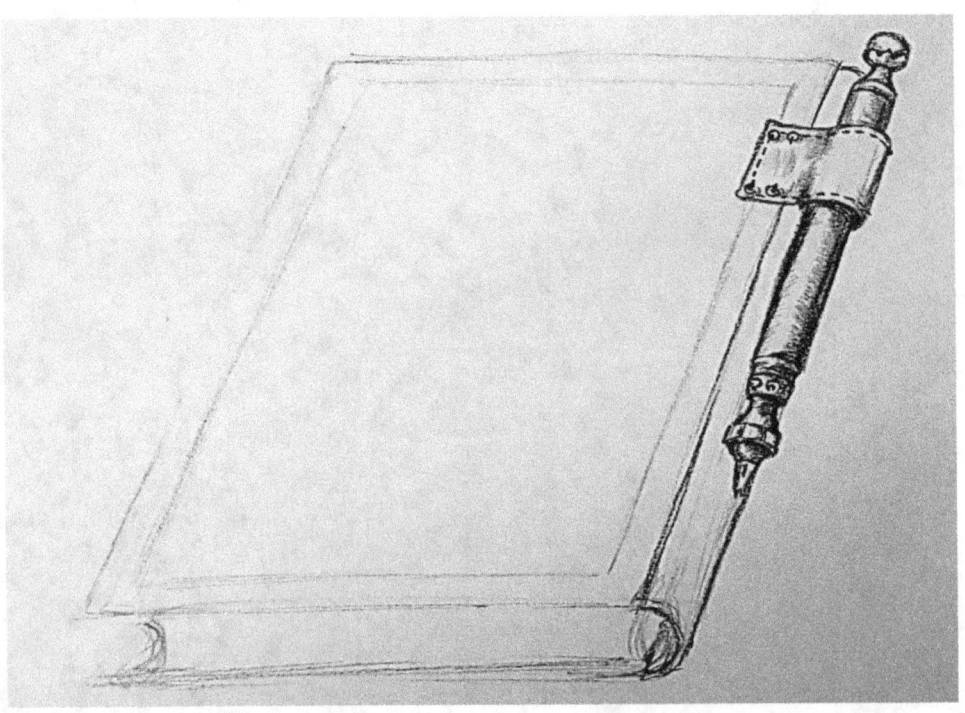

Step 4

Insert rivets to the border of the book cover. These rivets will be transformed into designs later. Draw the outline of two belts on the cover.

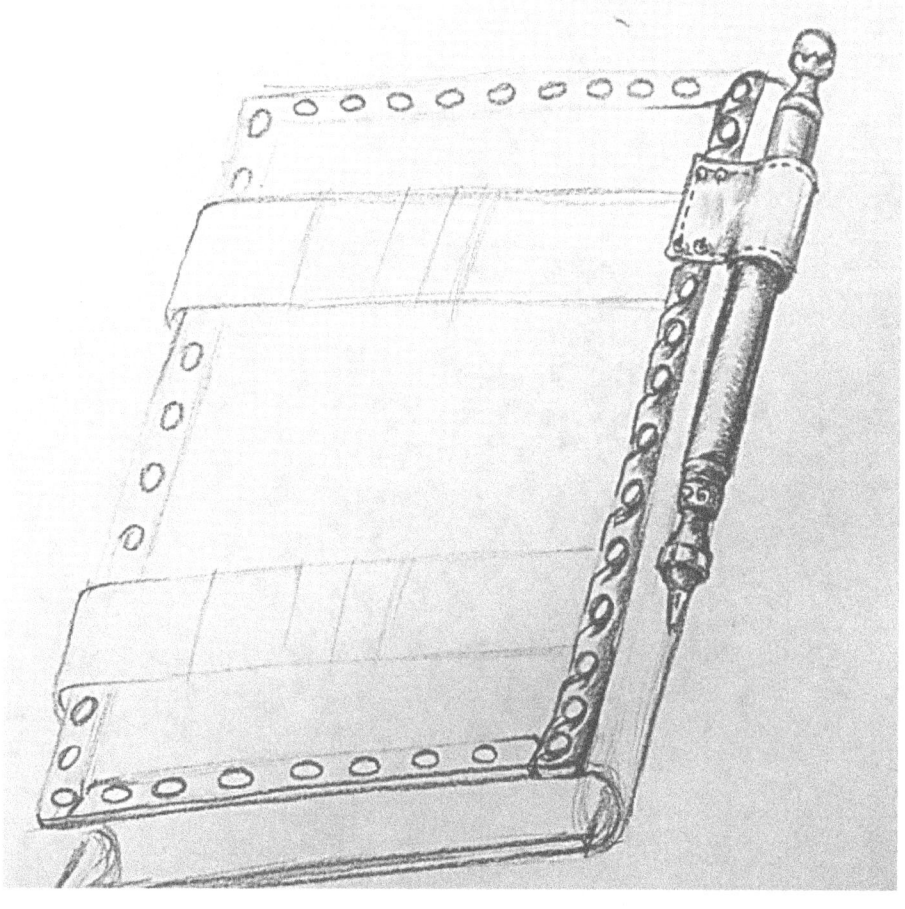

Step 5

Add buckles to the belts. Give a brief outline with some shading of a buckle with a loop, one each on both the belts.

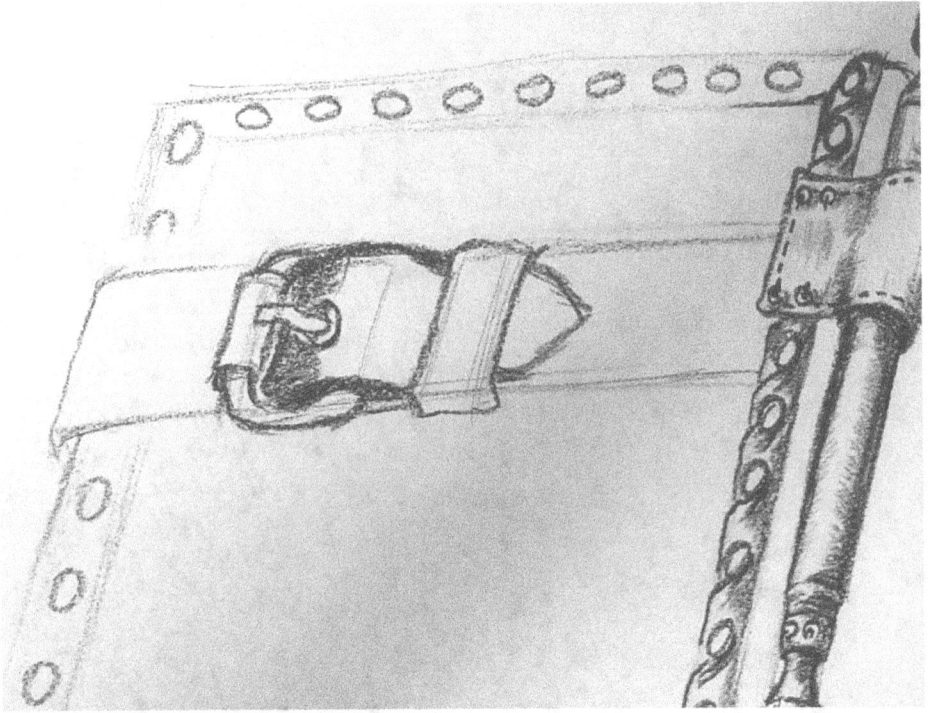

Step 6

Add stitches to the belts and give detailing to them. Notice the change in shading due to the curves in the belts. Carefully highlight the loop and the pin of the buckle. Add piercings to the belts and shade the rest of the area.

Begin shading the rivets along the border.

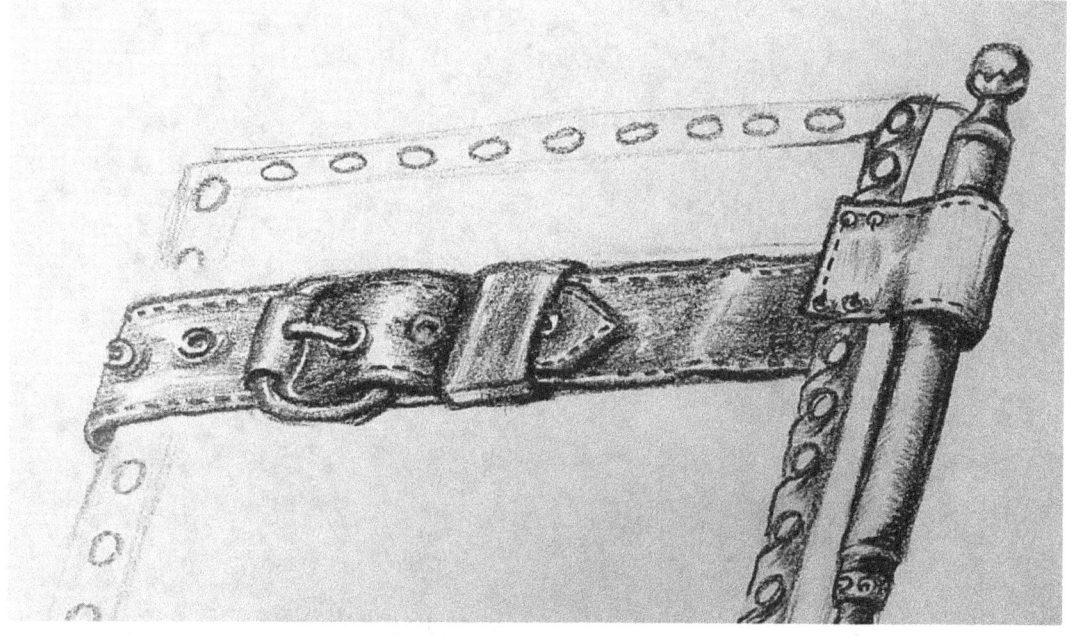

Step 7

Shade the rivets and design them like folded handmade embellishments on the border. The belts should come on top of the border. They should appear as if they are being used to hold the book to keep it closed.

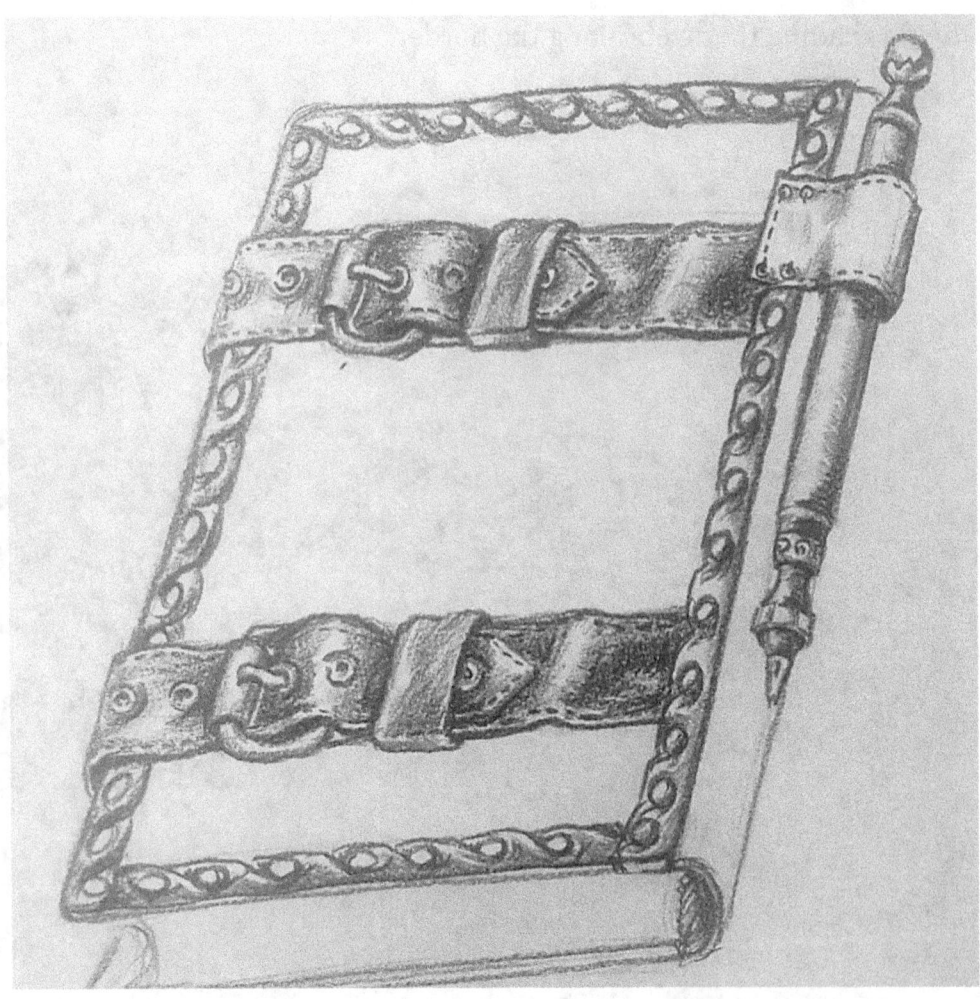

Step 8

Shade the pages that are visible from your perspective. Give details to the lower book cover. Its thickness should be highlighted with your shading. Notice the fine lines to depict the pages. Make them as realistic as possible. They are not just parallel lines. Make random lines-some short and some long. They look more appealing.

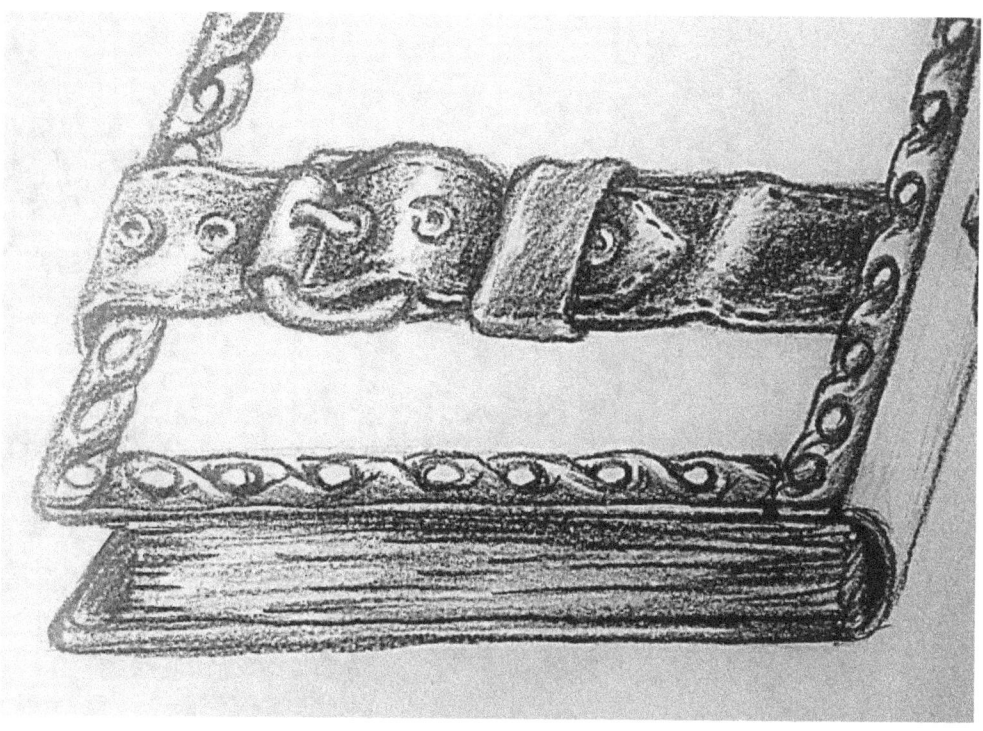

Step 9

Draw a wheel on the lower left corner of the book, underneath the belt. Make a spear coming out of the wheel heading diagonally towards the top right corner.

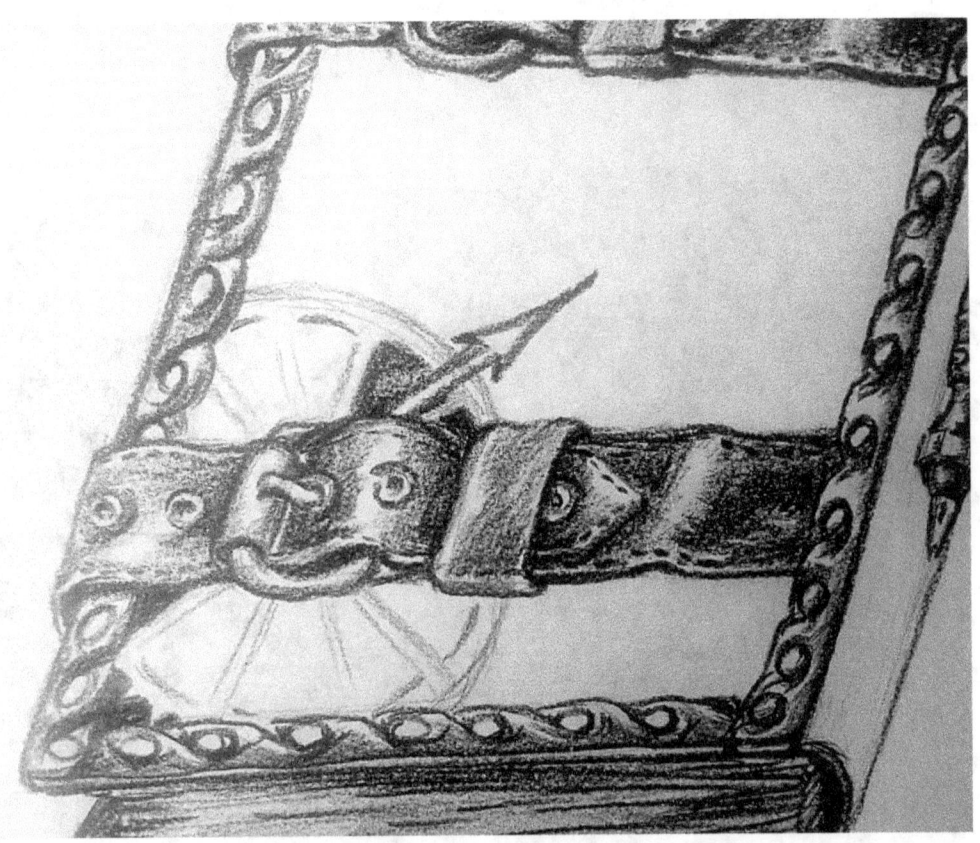

Step 10

Shade the wheel and the spear. The spokes of the wheel should be highlighted here.

Step 11

Now, to add the look of attachment of the pen with the book, make a spring or a spiral wire. This wire is attached to the pen as well as the top right corner of the book.

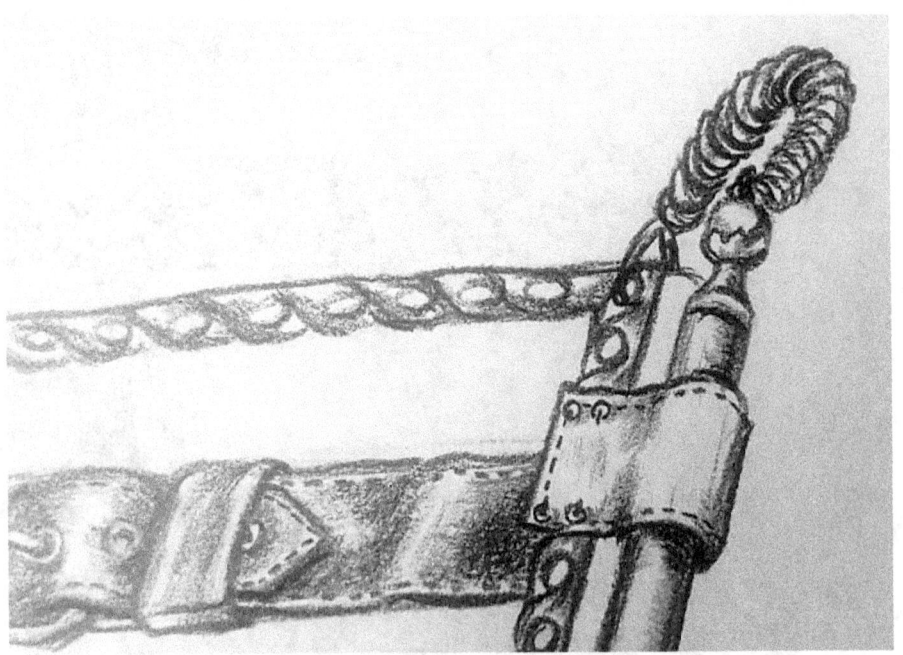

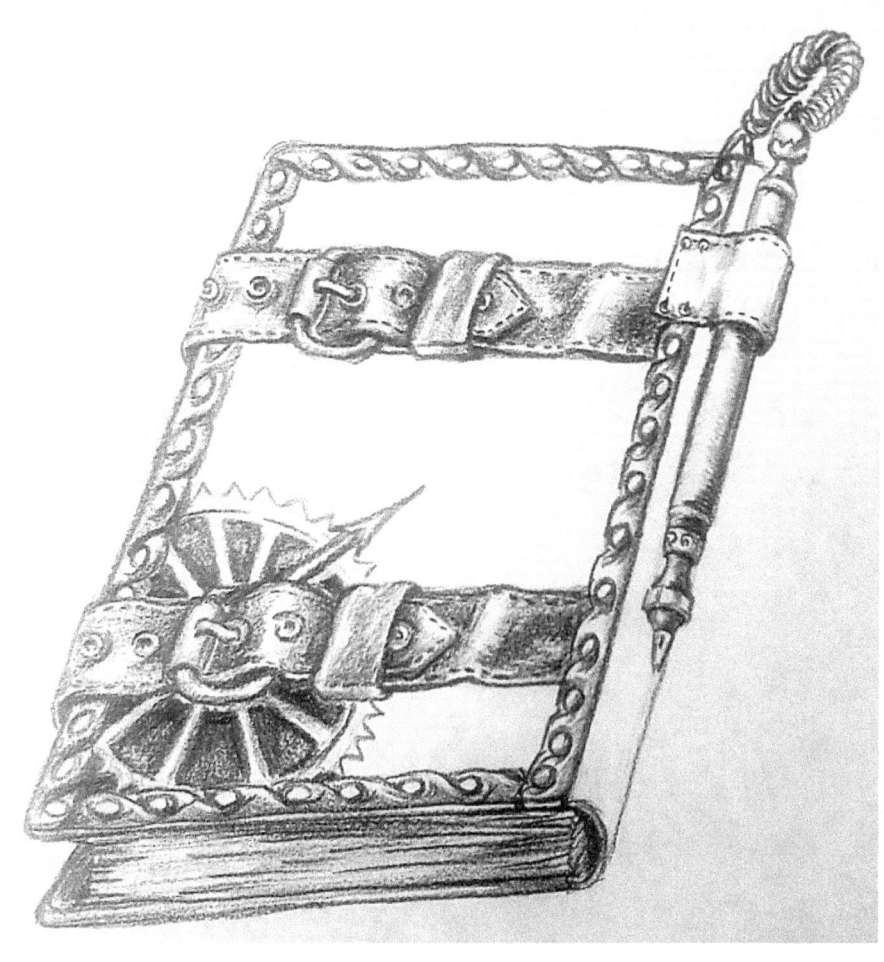

Step 12

Add teeth to the wheel, as we have done before in the drawing of gears.

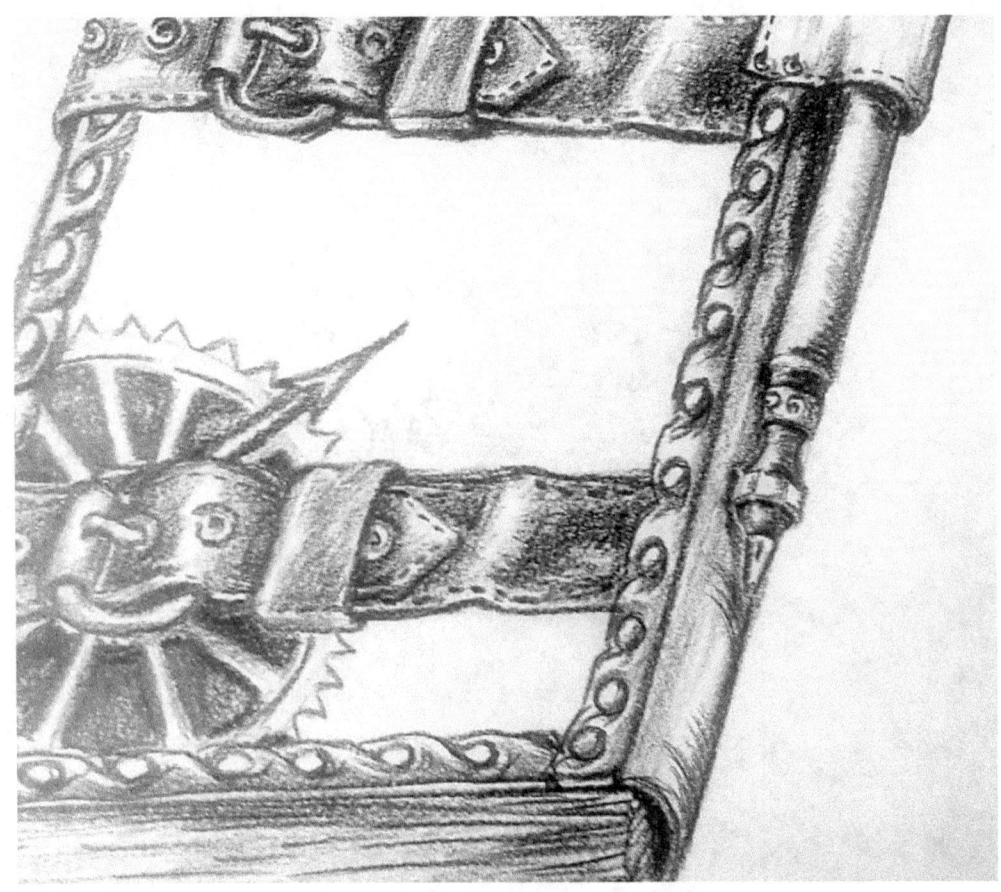

Step 13

We have to add another wheel near the previous wheel. Give the outline of a smaller wheel on top of the bigger one.

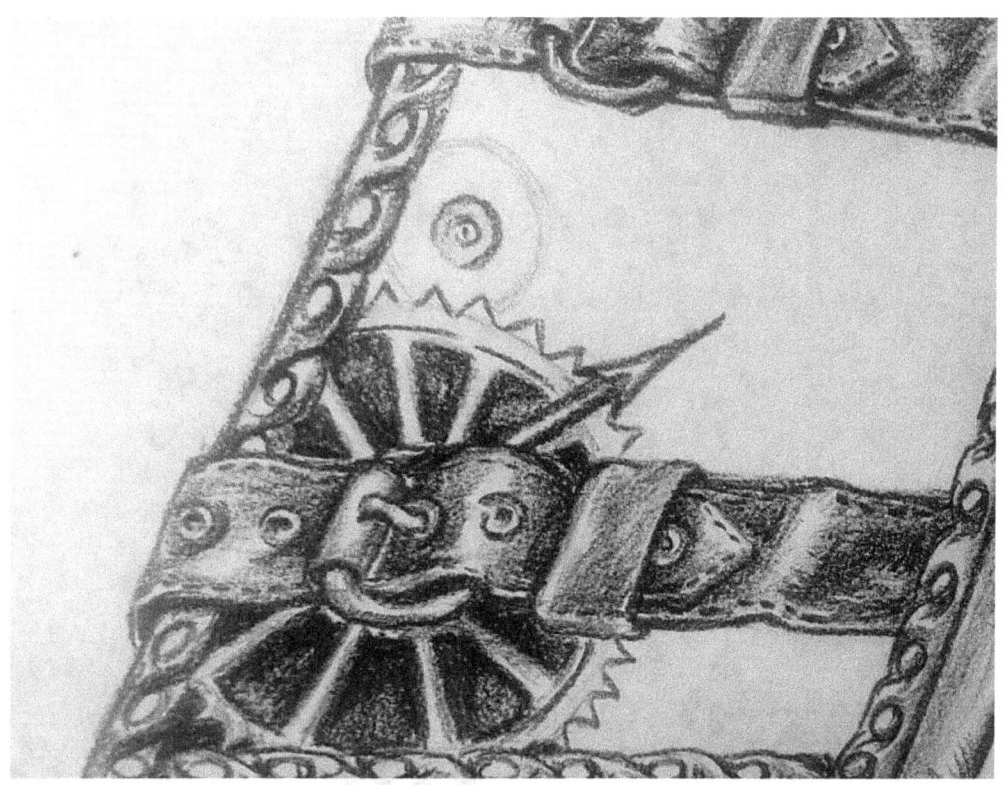

Step 14

Draw the spokes and shade the smaller wheel. Add outward curves to the outline of the smaller curve, surrounding its circumference.

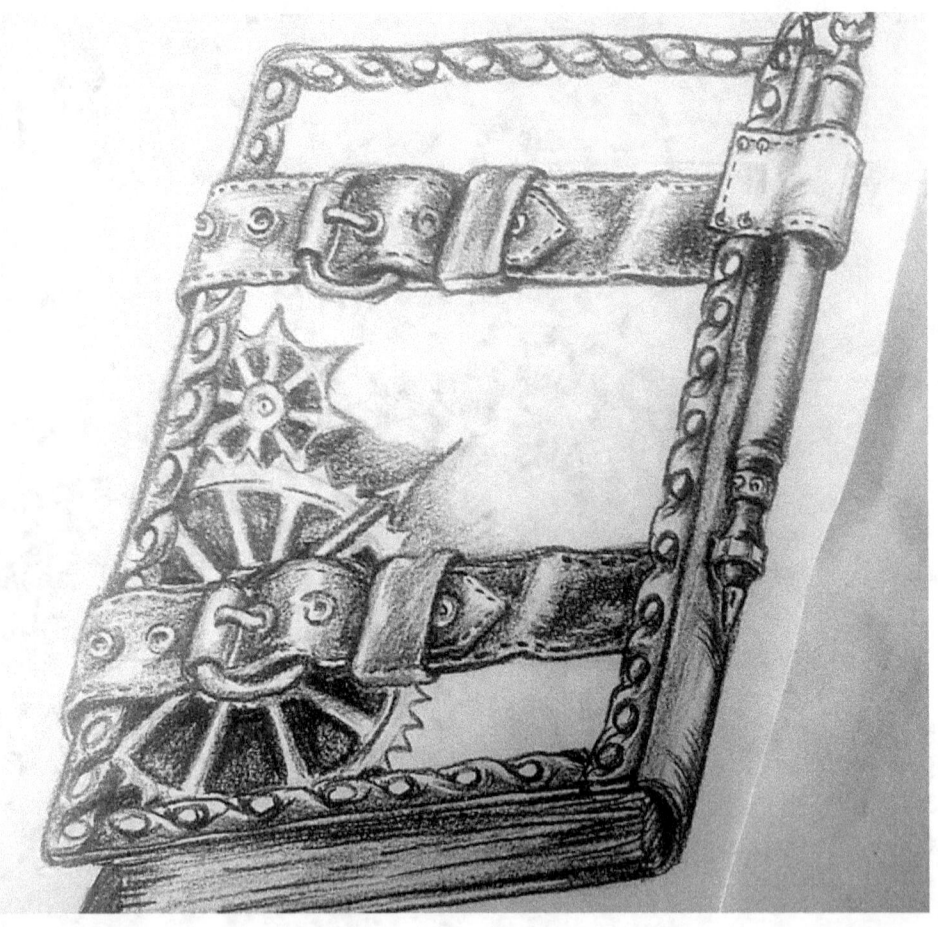

Step 15

We will draw a small latch on the cover of the book, attached with the help of a spiral wire, to the center of the smaller wheel. Draw the outline of the latch. It should look like an ancient lock.

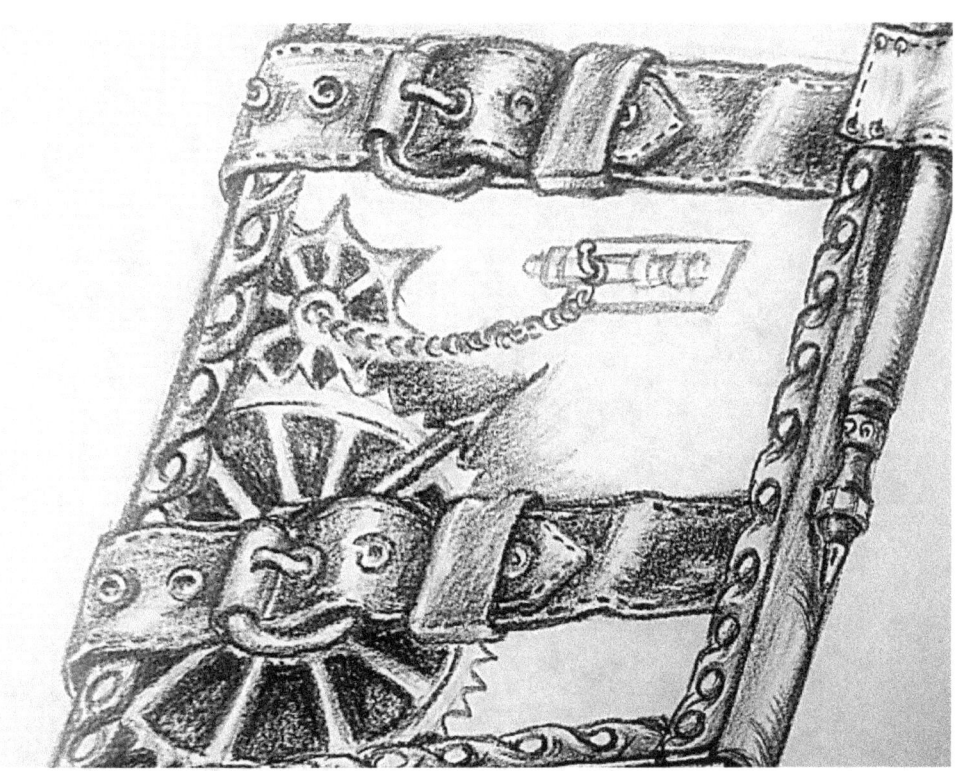

Step 16

Highlight the latch with darker lines and shading. Enhance the look of the attached spiral wire.

Step 17

Enhance the ancient look of the book by shading the remaining cover page gradually. Leave room for the shine that comes due to light reflection.

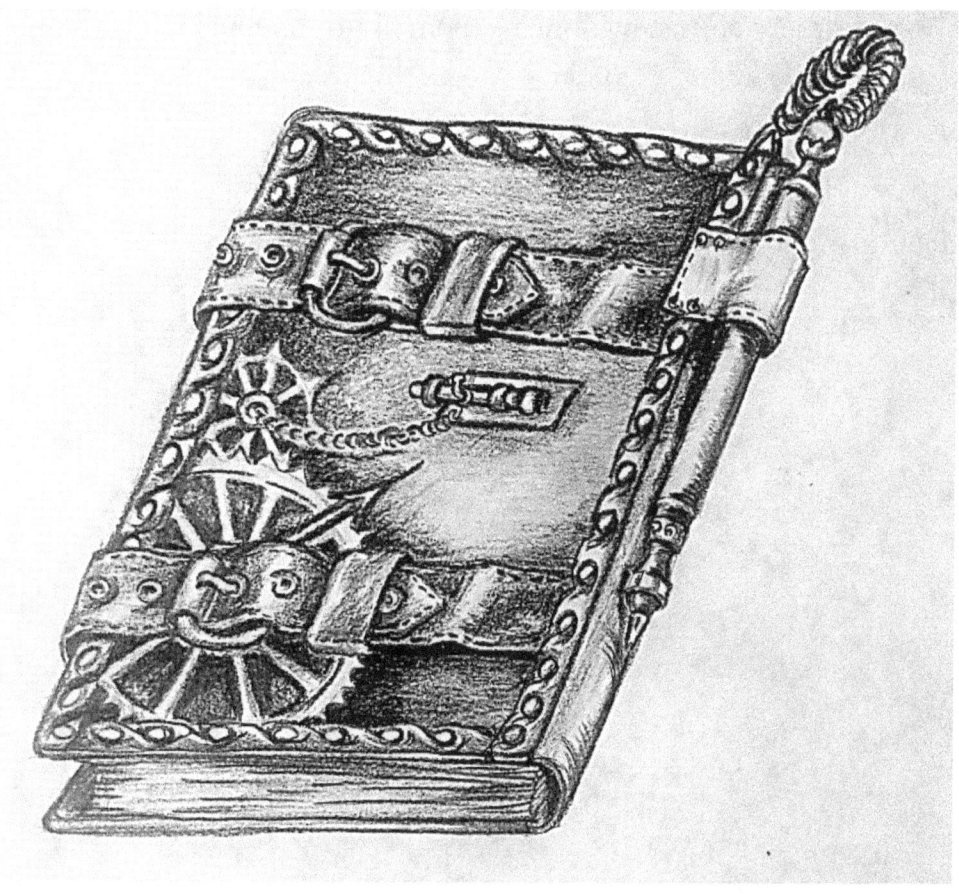

Step 18

Give finishing touches to the book, the pen and the latch by shading lighter and darker tones with pencil. Your ancient Steampunk book is ready.

Explore more objects by drawing them in this manner.

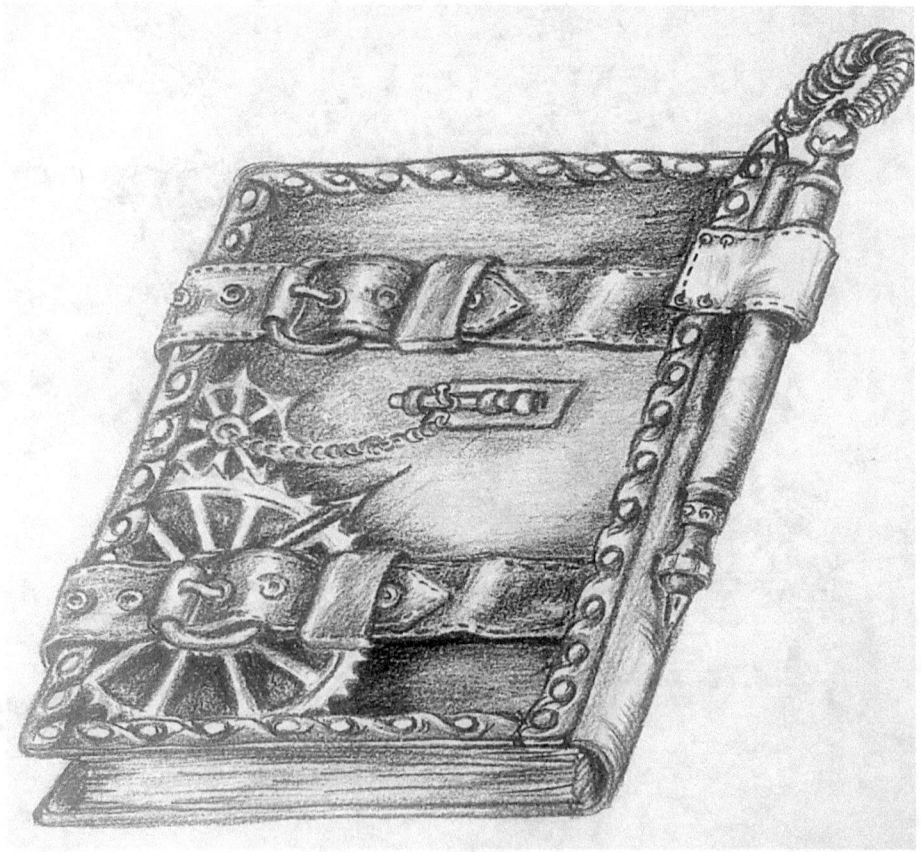

Conclusion

To a layman, Steampunk might be a completely new term. But the artists, who love to experiment in their work, this creative genre is a fantastic movement in the field of visual art. It is not at all difficult to master the drawings of this genre. Though they are intricate, they allow room for extensive creativity and imagination. You can get your hands on the shafts, bearings, ball bearings, fasteners, nuts, rivets, gears or cogwheels, gear trains, rack and pinion etc. with consistent practice. Once you have practiced enough, you will be able to transform any given object into a Steampunk object.

Some people might think that the sketching of machinery is a forte of male artists. But, it is not true. Many female artists are working extensively in this genre and have earned tremendous popularity. Steampunk artworks have been applied in the graphics as well as movies in the last few years. The popularity of this genre has broken all bounds in the extreme creative fields of visual art.

Having read the book- **STEAMPUNK-Drawing Amazing Steampunk Figures**, you must have got the idea of its basic drawing and shading. Keep practicing Steampunk figures and you will master this genre in just a few weeks.

Thank you!

Thank you for choosing our book, we hope you found it interesting and helpful.
If you liked the book, please give us a favor to write your review.

We would really appreciate this!

If you would like to have a bonus – **FREE BOOK**, please send the screenshot of your review to this e-mail:

kelly.artbooks@gmail.com and we will send you a **FREE BOOK** in PDF as a **GIFT!****

Hope to see you in our future books and good luck in your drawing experience!

** in the e-mail subject please mention the name of the book you reviewed and the author.

Other books by Jeffrey Stains

Steampunk:
Learn How to Draw
Amazing Steampunk Figures!
Book 2

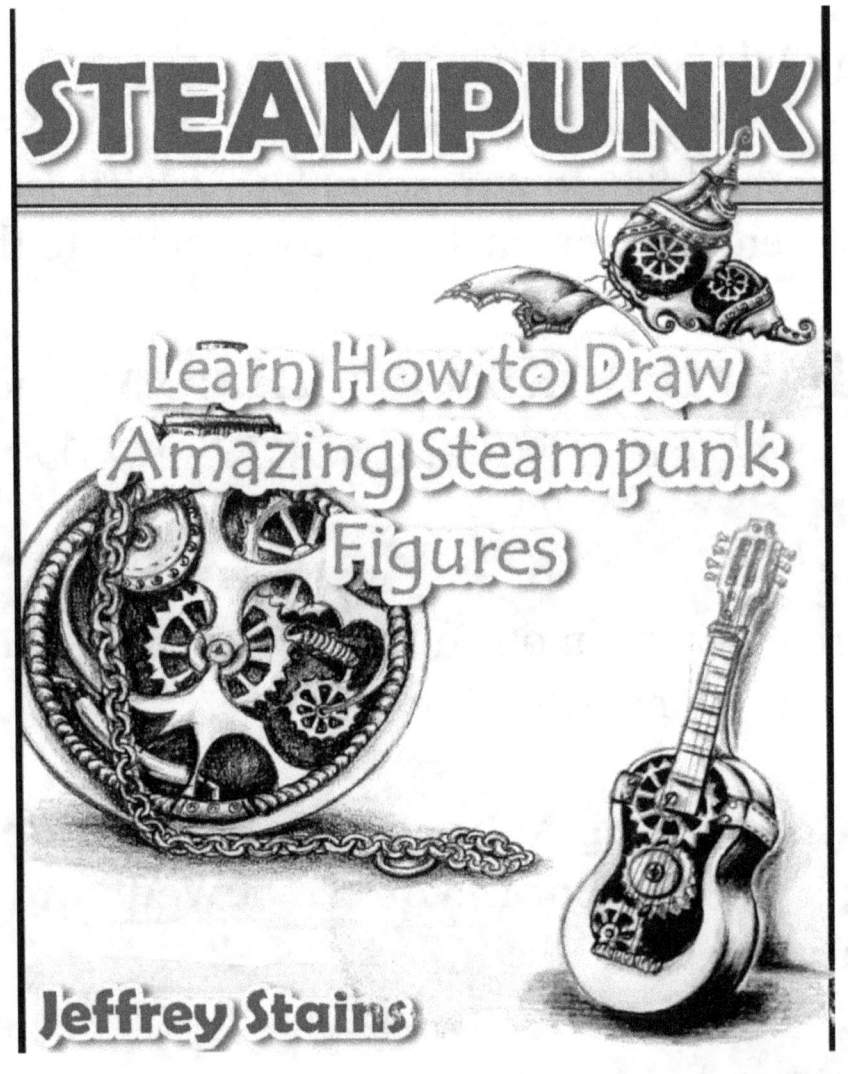

STEAMPUNK CATS Drawing:
A Completely New Form of Cats!

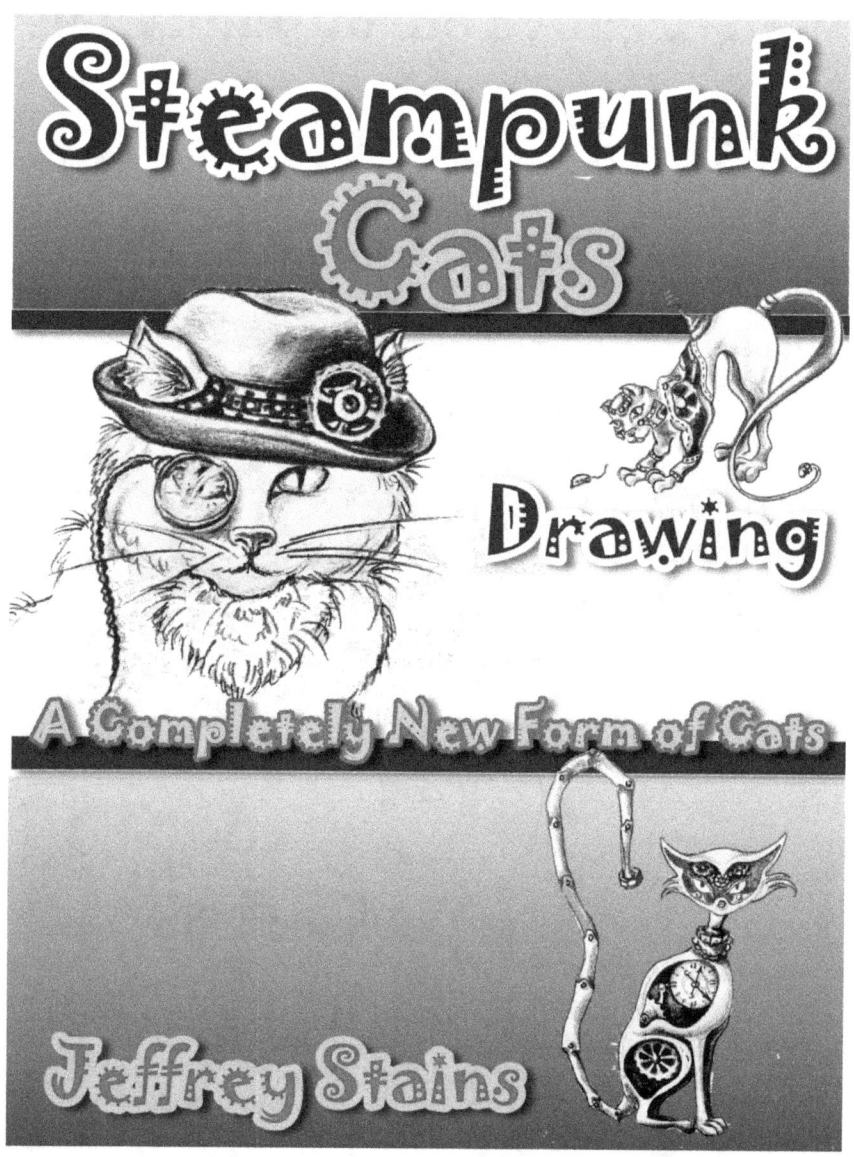

STEAMPUNK DOGS Drawing:

Unleash Your Imagination
with Creative Steampunk Dogs

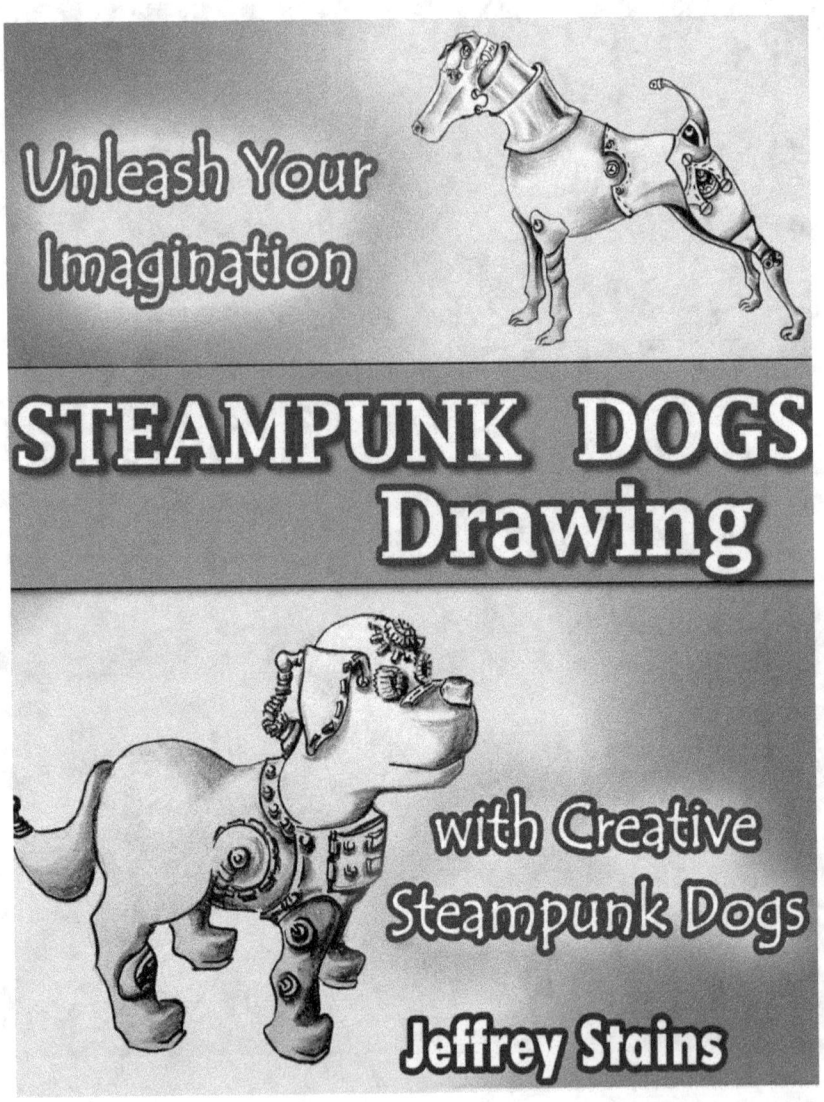

Steampunk Animals: Sketching Steampunk Animals with Creative Steampunk Drawings!

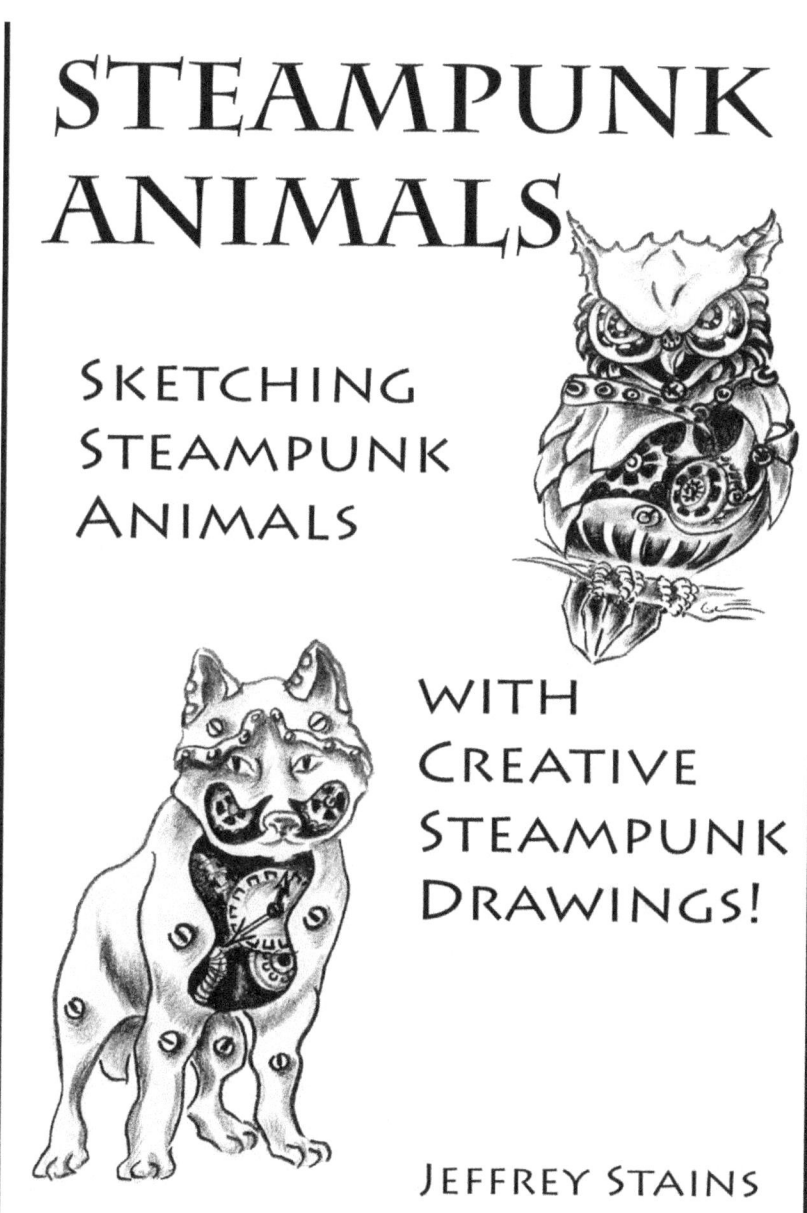

STEAMPUNK ANIMALS

SKETCHING STEAMPUNK ANIMALS

WITH CREATIVE STEAMPUNK DRAWINGS!

JEFFREY STAINS